New Level Pi

CW00858690

70-Day Life Transforming Prayer Project from Insightful Scriptures with 1,000 Inspired Prayers

----

By

Moses Gbenu

1

© New Level Prayer Handbook

(70-Day Life Transforming Prayer Project from Insightful Scriptures with 1,000 Inspired Prayers)

Life Publications, USA
www.lifepublications.org

Email: mosesgbenuola@gmail.com

Foreword

One major advantage we have as children of God is the privilege to pray to a God who has taken us as His children. He has given us the privilege to claim His Word and take the principles and revelations we have in His Word to pray. What a privilege to have a God who is a Father to us and who is ready to hear us!

However, prayer works better by our understanding of certain spiritual principles and our understanding of God. We can get such insights from His written Word, the Bible.

This book is a compilation of some of my weekly prayer bulletins which were being sent to a few of my friends through WhatsApp and a few editions on Facebook. Many of the recipients wrote to appreciate how much they have been blessed through the bulletins. Some used the prayer insights not only for their personal and family prayer times but also for their congregations, especially, their prayer meetings. Some of my friends prefer to use them for their night vigil prayers.

One common problem some of the recipients had was that their phones may crash or get lost and they lose the bulletins. On many occasions, I had to resend the back issues to such people.

Some of my friends, therefore, suggested that the bulletins be compiled into a book form that would make it more permanent and circulate wider.

That is the purpose for this book. It is my hope that this would be a blessing to every reader and also be an inspiration for a user to develop more prayers from the ones written here. This book is not intended to be a liturgy to be recited but a catalyst the Holy Spirit can use to inspire or generate personal prayers in our hearts as an outpouring of our spirits before our Father.

This is intended to be used continuously either daily or weekly as an individual may choose. I do not advise the reader to go through many prayer chapters at a time. It is not advisable to go through more than a session at a time.

Moses Gbenu

CONTENTS OF PRAYER CHAPTER-SESSIONS

Page No.

Introduction

This is not a book on a doctrine or a teaching on prayer. It is a book of prayers. It contains brief insightful expositions on some Bible passages. The passages are given as inspiration for the prayers the Holy Spirit has inspired me to generate from those passages. We pray by faith. But faith comes by hearing the Word of God. It is the revelation and understanding we have on a portion of Scripture that gives us the basis, the faith and the inspiration to pray and get results.

I will appeal to the reader not to just read this book, but to pray the book. This is not a story book that must be finished in a day, a week or to rush reading in any way. Each prayer session divided as chapters should be handled as a day's prayer session. A reader may even decide to treat a prayer chapter for a whole week or until he feels relieved in the spirit to go to the next prayer chapter. It is no achievement to finish the book 'in record time' and get little or no result.

It is advisable that when we have a prayer project, we should also have a prayer diary to record whatever idea or revelation or answers God gives in the course of such prayer project.

I trust God to change the spiritual landscape of every situation we bring on the table before the Lord in the course of this prayer sessions. Let me remind the reader that as a divine protocol, we don't jump into God's presence in prayers without thanksgiving and worship.

Prayer Session #1

I SHALL NOT CRY THIS YEAR

Text: 2 Kings: 4. 1-7

1. Now there cried a certain woman of the wives of the sons of the prophets unto Elisha, saying, Thy servant my husband is dead; and thou knowest that thy servant did fear the LORD: and the creditor is come to take unto him my two sons to be bondmen.

2. And Elisha said unto her, What shall I do for thee? Tell me, what hast thou in the house? And she said, Thine handmaid hath not anything in the house, save a pot of oil.

3. Then he said, Go, borrow thee vessels abroad of all thy neighbors, even empty vessels; borrow not a few.

4. And when thou art come in, thou shalt shut the door upon thee and upon thy sons, and shalt pour out into all those vessels, and thou shalt set aside that which is full.

5. So she went from him, and shut the door upon her and upon her sons, who brought the vessels to her; and she poured out.

6. And it came to pass, when the vessels were full, that she said unto her son, Bring me yet a vessel. And he said unto her, There is not a vessel more. And the oil stayed.

7. Then she came and told the man of God. And he said, Go, sell the oil, and pay thy debt, and live thou and thy children of the rest.

"The woman cried..."

#1. This year, I will not cry - over my spouse, over my children, over my job, over my health - in the name of Jesus Christ.

#2. In the name of Jesus, no one will cry over my life. I will not know pain; I will not know sorrow.

#3. Father, give no person any reason to commiserate with me this year - in the name of Jesus.

******

This man was one of the "sons of the prophets". He was a student in the school of prophets; and he died. This was a school of prophets which Samuel started. There were campuses in at least three cities – Bethel, Jericho and Jordan. This man was a student on one of the campuses. He was still training in the school of ministry. He had not graduated and had not started his own ministry when he suddenly died. By the new authority that Elisha had received from Elijah, he had become one of the faculty members of the school.

****

#4. In the name of Jesus Christ of Nazareth, I will not die while preparing for a greater tomorrow. I will not die unfulfilled. I will not die with my ministry and career dreams unfulfilled. I will not die while still in the school of ministry or in the process of learning, in the school of business or any career.

#5. No longer shall we lose any student on campus. As a church, fellowship or parish, we forbid the death of any student. We forbid the death of any of our young graduates. (Several have died through road accidents or terror attacks). Never again shall we lose any Christian student - in the name of Jesus!

#6. Any of our students or children or young graduates that are marked for death this year are released now and the death sentence is cancelled - in the name of Jesus.

#7. We will not lose any of our children who are students in any part of the world.

This woman said:

"Thy servant my husband is dead…"

#8. In the name of Jesus, this year my husband will not die. My wife will not die. I refuse to be a widow or widower this year.

"Thy servant … is dead."

#9. I will not die as a servant. Father, take me to a greater leadership position. I will not die at this level of my life. There is a level higher than where I am now. Give me a lifting this year - in the name of Jesus.

"…and thou knowest that thy servant feareth the LORD…"

The young prophet feared the LORD; but he still died.

Proverbs 10:27 says, *"The fear of the LORD prolongeth days; but the years of the wicked shall be shortened."*

#10. Father, because I fear you, I refuse to die in the midst of my days. No sickness, accident or any form of attack will shorten my days – in the name of Jesus.

11

#11. I bring all my children under the covenant of protection. No evil shall befall any of us this year.

#12. Jehovah Rapha, if there is any health condition in my body that is capable of terminating my life this year, Father, let Your mercy prevail over this and heal me – in the name of Jesus.

#13. Any process of damage or decay that is going on in my body that is capable of sending me to the untimely grave, Father, stop the process - in the name of Jesus. (Please, pray these two similar prayers and #14 well before you move to #15).

#14. When Hezekiah had a sickness and was to die in his late 40s, he reminded You of His walk with You and You delivered him from a terminal disease. Father, remember my walk with You over the years and lengthen my days. Have mercy on me. Let me not expire in the midst of my days – in the name of Jesus.

Proverbs 19:23 says, *"The fear of the Lord tendeth to life; and he that hath it shall abide satisfied: he shall not be visited with evil."*

#15. Father, in the midst of a dangerous and wicked generation and society, I shall not be visited with evil - evil on highway, evil in the streets, evil in the house in the midnight, evil in brought daylight.

#16. The 'pestilence that walketh in darkness' or the 'destruction that goes about in the noon day' shall not move near me or my family members. (Psalm 91:5-6).

#17. I am secure from the snares of satanic fowlers, and secure from dangerous pestilences.

#18. You will cover me with Your feathers. You shall remain my shield and my buckler.

#19. No sponsored arrow flying by night will hit me or my spouse or children. (Psalm 91:5).

#20. No human or spiritual pestilence that walks about in the night will move near me.

#21. I will escape natural disasters and community calamities.

#22. My wife/husband shall not be visited with evil.

#23. My children will not be visited with evil. #

This prophet died leaving two young boys behind.

#24. Father, my children will not become fatherless or motherless early in life. (Don't wait till you are married and have children before you pray such prayers. Prayer is an investment.)

#25. No one will be a representative father or mother to my children - in the name of Jesus.

#26. I declare in the name of Jesus Christ, that no one will represent me on the day of my children's glory.

(If already, your spouse is late, say, "Father, raise great fathers for my children from nations of the world - in the name of Jesus.")

#27. In the name of Jesus, I will not break down before my breakthrough.

#28. My spouse will not break down.

#29. Any untimely death programmed for me is terminated.

#30. I silence any voice calling me from the grave – in the name of Jesus.

#31. My body, my body: you will not answer any invitation from the grave this year - in the name of Jesus!

#32. Any hidden curse or covenant of untimely death in my life - expire - in the name of Jesus!

#33. In the church of God, we banish the scourge of breast cancer among middle age women.

#34. We banish every form of cancer among our men - in the name of Jesus.

#35. We cancel any death already programmed for any of our ministers this year - in the name of Jesus.

#36. Father, we thank You because in You we live and move and have our being.

#37. Father, service our bodies to live for you and serve you.

#38. With long life you will satisfy us and show us Your salvation.

****

This prophet of 2 Kings 4 had no partner in ministry who could take care of his children after his death. His ministry probably died with him.

When Jesus was to die, He handed over His mother to a great partner in ministry (John 19:25-27). And handed over the ministry to partners who made sure the work continues till today! (Mark 16:15-20).

****

#39. Father, give me men - who can give me what I need.

#40. Father, Give me women - who have what I lack.

#41. Blessed be the name of the Lord.

Prayer Session #2

MY CHILDREN SHALL NOT BE SERVANTS

2 Kings: 4. 1-7. Read this passage again.

"The woman said, the creditor is come to take unto him my two sons to be bondmen."

#1. Lord, I thank You this day You have made. I will rejoice and be glad in it.

#2. I will enter my rest - in marriage, in career, in business, in ministry, in my body; I will experience your Sabbath. My children will enjoy your rest, your Sabbath.

#3. My children will not become bondmen or bondwomen in strange lands or in their places of nativity.

Today, many African young men and women have become bondwomen and men in the Arab world, Europe and all over the world. Even in Africa, many are slaves to Chinese, Lebanese and Indian oppressors.

#4. My seed will not suffer in his country or outside his country.

#5. My children shall all become employers of labor - in the name of Jesus. (Don't pray this if you don't believe in this).

****

15

Our father, Abraham, was an employer of labor, so was Isaac and so was Jacob. It is difficult to be wealthy as a lifelong employee. As an employee, the inherited covenant blessings on Jacob were being enjoyed mainly by his employer, Laban. Jacob continued to suffer until he had his own portion of the business.

****

#6. My seed will not be slaves to men - in the name of Jesus. (Mention them by name)

#7. Any spiritual ancestral creditor waiting to hold my children for ransoms in any area of life, I revoke the debts - in the name of Jesus.

#8. By the blood of Jesus, I release my children from any ancestral hidden debts. (Mention their names. If you don't have a child yet, pray in advance),

> Verse 2. ***And Elisha said unto her, 'What shall I do for thee?'***

#9. Father, raise for me MEN and WOMEN who will be eager and enthusiastic to help me.

#10. Raise for me people who have answers to my needs; men and women who have answers to my prayers, men and women who have what I need and people who need what I have.

> ***"...what hast thou in the house? And she said, Thine handmaid hath not anything in the house, save a pot of oil."***

#11. Father, open my eyes to see what I have in the house or in my life that You can use as raw materials for miracles to change my history.

#12. Lord, I hand over my pot of oil to you. Use it to make something out of my life.

16

****

No child of God is empty. There is always 'a pot of oil', a remnant, an 'except' - that is left - that God can use to bring a new beginning. Assyria invaded and carried away thousands of Jews as slaves in Israel. But there were remnants. Nebuchadnezzar came and slaughtered thousands and carried away thousands from Judah. But there was a remnant. Hitler roasted 6 million Jews. But some remnants escaped. Those that escaped are the controllers of the banking industry in America today and the recipients of the highest number of Nobel Laurels in the world.

****

#13. Father, no matter what the enemy has destroyed or stolen from my life, use my remnants to bless me and give me something greater than what I have lost.

#14. No matter how much backsliding and treachery and spiritual bankruptcy going on in the church of God today globally, there are still remnants. Father, use the remnants in Your House in this nation with the little pot of oil we have to cause a national revival of righteousness-in the name of Jesus.

#15. Father, I pray for every member of this House (your own church or ministry) who may be experiencing any embarrassing situation at the moment to receive help from above - in the name of Jesus.

#16. All those carrying one debt burden or the other, Father do one major miracle to settle this - in the name of Jesus. Open new doors of business or opportunities for them.

#17. Some people thought this widow was finished because the breadwinner is dead. Father, let all those who think it is finished with me, come and celebrate with me very soon.

#18. I pray for our brethren who have lost their spouses - that Heaven will arise and bless them supernaturally, provide for them what their late spouses could not provide.

#19. Let God give them a new beginning and wipe away their tears permanently – in the name of Jesus.

****

"Then he said, Go, borrow thee vessels abroad of all thy neighbors, even empty vessels; borrow not a few."

Borrowing is not necessarily bad. It depends on the purpose, the conditions and the demands of the lender. Sometimes, borrowing can be the best or only option available to raise you up in life or to give you a new beginning.

God's servant instructed the widow to go and borrow. Jesus too borrowed two donkeys to ride to Jerusalem to fulfill a prophecy on His life. He was dignified that day. Those celebrating Him did not ask Him whether or not He bought the donkeys. They honored Him. He was to die in a few days and didn't have to buy a new vehicle. The lenders of the donkeys didn't ask for any collateral or guarantors. His name was a guarantee.

The prophet that died probably borrowed money to pay rent or to eat.

****

#20. Father, I will not borrow money to eat. Let me never borrow food to feed my family.

****

Jesus gave a parable of a man who had a visitor in the middle of the night. The host had no food in the house, no cooked food in the fridge and no foodstuff to prepare. He had to go and borrow food from his neighbor around 12 became a nuisance to his neighbor, knocking continuously and crying "Friend, lend me three loaves (Luke 11:5).

****

#21. In the name of Jesus, I will not borrow to eat. I will not borrow to entertain a guest.

#22. My guests will not see my lack. I will not suffer financial shame or embarrassment.

The widow borrowed vessels - containers - equipment - to start a business. Borrowing to start a business is good if the business is good and the market is there waiting for you. There are many of us with great ideas, but no resources to execute.

You are looking for people to either give you the money or lend you the capital and nobody is ready to do it. You approach a bank and they say, "Go and bring your grandmother's marriage certificate" or some ridiculous things as collateral!

****

#23. Father, grant me favor. Everywhere I go to ask for help, let me receive favor – in the name of Jesus.

#24. Father, give unto me everything I need - material and money - to start or expand my business - in the name of Jesus.

****

*"Go, borrow thee vessels abroad of **all thy neighbors,** even empty vessels; borrow not a few."*

What if the woman wasn't on good terms or in good relationship with her neighbors?

19

t even ask what she wanted to do with
ney trusted her. They had never suspected
f she always quarreled in the neighborhood
people, nobody would have lent her their

ave earned bad reputation in our neighborhood
and o.. cause of our poor relationship with neighbors.

Look at the lenders who gave Jesus the donkeys. All they heard
was "the Lord hath need of them" and they immediately
released those two donkeys. Do you have a good name,
integrity and reputation to borrow?

****

#25. Father, where my name or reputation has suffered,
redeem it - in the name of Jesus.

#26. Give me grace to do what is needful to redeem my image.

#27. Lord, give me a name that is marketable, a name that is
respectable everywhere.

****

Do you have any request pending on someone's table? Let the
Lord grant you favor and let the request be granted - in the
name of Jesus.

"...all thy neighbors..."

It was ALL the neighbors of the widow that gave this woman
their empty vessels. No single neighbor rejected her request.

****

#29. From today, no one shall say No to me. Whoever has
what I need shall release it on request. Lord, grant me this
special favor in the name of Jesus. #

In Egypt, all the Egyptians that Israelites approached to ask for gold and silver released their gold - even though they knew Israel would soon leave Egypt!

****

#30. My Egyptians will release their gold without asking questions - in the name of Jesus.

#31. Lord, give me new neighbors with vessels, new friends, new Egyptians with gold, new donkey owners - who have what I need and who are eager to release them without any suicidal strings or ropes attached.

#32. Thank the Lord for taking you to another level.

Prayer Session #3

LORD, GIVE ME NEIGHBORS!

2 Kings 4:2-7

> 2. *And Elisha said unto her, What shall I do for thee? tell me, what hast thou in the house? And she said, Thine handmaid hath not any thing in the house, save a pot of oil.*
>
> 3. *Then he said, Go, borrow thee vessels abroad of all thy neighbors, even empty vessels; borrow not a few.*
>
> 4. *And when thou art come in, thou shalt shut the door upon thee and upon thy sons, and shalt pour out into all those vessels, and thou shalt set aside that which is full.*
>
> 5. *So she went from him, and shut the door upon her and upon her sons, who brought the vessels to her; and she poured out.*
>
> 6. *And it came to pass, when the vessels were full, that she said unto her son, Bring me yet a vessel. And he said unto her, "There is not a vessel more". And the oil stayed.*
>
> 7. *Then she came and told the man of God. And he said, Go, sell the oil, and pay thy debt, and live thou and thy children of the rest.*

Elisha told the widow she should borrow empty vessels from *"ALL thy neighbors"*

We don't know how many neighbors the woman had. But the wine production stopped at the number of vessels she borrowed. The anointing for more oil production was still available. But the oil stopped because there were no more vessels. The anointing was underutilized. Maybe the woman didn't get to ALL her neighbors. Maybe she didn't have many neighbors. Maybe she selected just a few of the women she could relate with.

Her oil production output and continued production were not determined by her capital, raw material input or staff strength. Her production and profit were determined by the number of neighbors she had.

****

#1. Lord, give me a character and wisdom that can attract many clients, more friends, many more neighbors, many more supporters and partners than I have at the moment.

(Pray this prayer very well before you move on).

#2. Jesus said part of the promises of blessings of forsaking all to follow Him are, *"hundred fold brothers, hundred fold sisters, hundred fold mothers, hundred fold fathers..."* (Mark 10:30).

#3. Lord Jesus, these are part of the promises You gave me in Your Word: Give me hundred-fold fathers - people who will be concerned about me as real fathers; those who will have a father's burden to pray and fast for me secretly without any string attached. It means that even in the kingdom of God alone, there is enough market for your product and services.

****

Do you have products or services? Elisha told the woman,

"Go, sell the oil and pay the debts..."

Who were the clients or customers for the oil? The same neighbors who lent out their vessels. If the woman had asked them to give her money to pay her debts, they might not have. But they brought the same money they should have given her to buy something produced by her through their vessels!

It was the same neighbors that the woman sold the oil to.

****

#4. Father, give me buying neighbors, purchasing neighbors - men and women looking for my product and services, men and women looking for my ability; men and women who have enough money to pay for these; men and women looking for my ministry.

***

The neighbors had vessels and some oil too; but they had no anointing to multiply their own oil. They lent their vessels out because the vessels were empty and under-utilized. Now they had to be coming to the Widow to be buying oil regularly.

***

#5. Father, give me an anointing and grace that will give me an advantage over my neighbors and colleagues - neighbors in the same industry, neighbors in the same profession, in the same market, in the same community.

"Neighbors" don't have to be the people in your immediate environment. Neighbors can come from across the seas. Elijah did not limit the widow's neighbors to a specific geographical location. But the woman could have limited herself. The prophet said,

24

"....Go, borrow thee vessels ABROAD of all thy neighbors,"

Another translation says, "...EVERYWHERE..."

If your neighbors do not extend beyond your street, you may not go far in life, business or ministry.

***

#6. Father, give me neighbors abroad, neighbors across the seas and across the deserts; neighbors from everywhere, neighbors in Africa, neighbors from Europe, Asia and Americas - in the name of Jesus.

***

Speaking of the ministry of John the Baptist, the Bible says,

> *"Then went out to him Jerusalem, and ALL Judea and ALL the region round about Jordan ... Confessing their sins"* (Matt 3:5-6).

There was nothing physically attractive in John and his location of ministry headquarters.

But "Jerusalem" went to John. That means everybody in the city. "And ALL Judea" went to him.

This is not normal. At that time, Bethabara beyond Jordan River where John was doing ministry was about 12km from the city of Jerusalem. And people walked down there.

Later, Jesus asked the multitudes concerning John,

> *"...What went ye out into the wilderness for to see? A reed shaken with the wind? But what went ye out for to see? A man clothed in soft raiment? Behold, they which are gorgeously*

25

appareled, and live delicately, are in kings courts.
26 But what went ye out for to see? A prophet? Yea, I say unto you, and much more than a prophet." (Luke 7:24-26)

John had no physical attraction, no fine church building, no miracles or healings. His dress wasn't attractive. His jacket was of the skin of camel. He doesn't have to change it for years or even dry-clean it or iron it. But multitudes were rushing to him IN THE WILDERNESS. There was something in him that was attracting ALL the neighbors far and near. Jesus said, those who are gorgeously dressed are in the palace. John's dress was appalling, not appealing. But there was a grace on him attracting even those in the palaces to seek his audience and look for the services he was offering in the wilderness. Even his product (his message) wasn't attractive. But his neighbors came for it.

***

#7. Father, let your grace upon my life begin to attract men and women.

***

A man, Pastor Enoch Adeboye, went to build a house in a wilderness and built a little shed there for prayer meetings. Today, it is almost like "ALL Jerusalem..." go there. People come from all over the world to pray there. No matter the size of auditorium he motivates the church to build, 'neighbors' will fill it before the auditorium is finished. There is a grace attracting people. It is not publicity, it is not even prayer (he is not the one praying most in the world) and it is more than anointing. There is a grace behind that.

Because of his presence there, hundreds of thousands of people have left Lagos to come and be his permanent neighbors in the Camp and all around. Several villages and communities have sprung up around the Camp which has now become a city. Pieces of land that were not worth more than N20,000 ($400) per plot a few years ago now sell for several millions in the neighborhood.

In fact, most of our successes are determined by the number of neighbors and the kind of neighbors we attract. If you have a website or blog and there are no 'neighbors' visiting, it will die! If you have a tweeter page and have 3 million followers or a YouTube channel with millions of viewers and subscribers - that becomes a big market for your ideas, product and services and ministry message. Once you have many neighbors, Google would pay you because they would advertise to your neighbors.

If you apply to big time publishers to publish your material, they would want to find out how many 'neighbors' you have – the number of people who are your friends and following you on social media like Facebook, Tweeter, etc.

***

#8. I pray for you in your new location of business or ministry. Heaven will bring your neighbors from far and near, the neighbors that need your ministry, your message, your ideas, your services, your products, God will bring them to you. Your life, ministry and business will begin to attract new attention - in the name of Jesus. (Pray this into your life again.)

***

"Go, sell the oil and pay thy debts ..."

In Nigeria, God has given us plenty of oil. Our oil is flowing every day and many vessels are being loaded every day. We have been selling this oil every day for about 60 years and yet we are accumulating huge debts.

Those who are selling our oil and not paying debts, God will deliver us from them - in the name of Jesus. We are accumulating debts. Despite our oil, we have budget deficits of trillions of Naira. Many state governments owe huge debts locally and externally. Yet we are selling oil - every day!

***

#9. As a citizen of Nigeria (or anywhere you are from), Father, in the name of Jesus, I make a demand on the oil and other wealth of my nation.

#10. As the oil of Nigeria (or your nation) continues to flow and neighbors are coming from ABROAD to buy, I make a demand on my allocation.

#11. I refuse to remain in any form of debt. I will begin to enjoy the oil and other mineral wealth of this nation - in the name of Jesus!

#12. All those who have plundered our oil wealth and those presently doing so shall be plundered - in the name of Jesus.

#13. My nation will not collapse under debt burdens.

#14. Our sons and daughters who have become slaves to our creditors overseas and in their own lands shall be restored in dignity. Every legitimate citizen of this country shall be dignified everywhere in the world. No longer shall our sons be associated with evil.

#15. As global citizens, I make a demand on the wealth of nations.

***

If possible, continue to pray these prayers or add more for more days as the Holy Spirit helps you.

*"Now there **cried** a certain woman of the wives of the sons of the prophets **unto Elisha**..."*

By crying to Elisha, the woman was making a demand on the anointing on the life of the man of God. She was not asking for money. She knew Elisha had no money. He had left his farming business, resigned his directorship and had been living by faith. To be a prophet in those days wasn't fashionable or financially attractive. The woman's husband had died in debt. He was a prophet-in-training. He was in a college of prophets where the hostel facilities were poor. This was a college where several students were sleeping in the same room (2 Kings 6:1) and where feeding was difficult (2 Kings 4:38-41). Who knows what killed this young prophet? It could have been hunger or malnutrition. It could be a health condition that he had no money to treat.

If you don't respect the grace of God upon a man of God, it may not benefit you. The widow didn't pray TO Elisha. It was simply a demand on the anointing on his life. We must not worship or venerate a preacher. But we can make a demand on the anointing on a man's life. When you kneel down and ask a man to pray for you, you are not kneeling to the man but making a demand on the anointing on his life. If you despise a preacher, his anointing won't work for you. Scripture says, "Believe in the Lord your God and you shall be established; believe in His prophets and you shall prosper." (2 Chronicles 20:20b). You may believe in God and be a nice Christian. But if you despise a man of God who is indeed a genuine man of God, the grace of God upon him may not work for you.

The woman of the issue of blood made a demand on the anointing on Jesus and his garment. Other people were touching Jesus and his garment, but because there was no demand in their touch, virtue did not flow towards their direction.

Choose a man of God you respect, a man of integrity and power, a man who has good testimony even among unbelievers as a genuine prophet.

Make a demand on the specific grace of God you have found operating in his life. He may not be your direct pastor, but God can use him to be a blessing to you.

Prayer Session #4

DELIVERANCE FROM UNKNOWN COLLATERALS

(Securing our lives and those of our children from Hidden Spiritual Debts)

Back to: 2 Kings: 4. 1

> *1. Now there cried a certain woman of the wives of the sons of the prophets unto Elisha, saying, Thy servant my husband is dead; and thou knowest that thy servant did fear the LORD: and the creditor is come to take unto him my two sons to be bondmen....*

The prophet borrowed money to solve an immediate problem; but his two boys were the collateral. He probably had no personal property. If he had a property, the creditor would have claimed this. The boys were the only collateral available. The boys didn't know there was a loan burden they inherited. Their mother too probably didn't know the full implications of the loan until the creditor came knocking. She may not even have known there was such loan.

Many of our own fathers and grandfathers or grandmothers have made some transactions with certain spiritual creditors - to get quick access to money, success in business, protection from enemies, long life, fame, political power, religious power to divine, to heal or receive healing, to see things in the spirit, to commune with spirits, to have children, to attract or force love, etc. Often, the children or grandchildren are the collateral and they are usually oblivious to this until the spiritual creditor begins to make demands.

For some of us, our ancestors have spent our money in advance. They have taken money from satanic 'finance houses' and we are the collateral.

In my book, *Deliverance from Voluntary and Pleasurable Bondage,* I gave the following story:

> Suffering from abject poverty, a sister went to ask her grandmother some questions. Why is it that even though she and her siblings were well educated and intelligent and yet poor? Highly connected to great men, but nothing comes from their connections. The old woman revealed that when she was younger, she made a charm to be rich and successful in her restaurant business. When the charm started working, she could cook 8 bags of rice and sell all in a day! If you passed by the restaurant, something would draw you inside to eat. If you ate once, you must come back again and you may not be easily satiated by your normal quantity. If you were living in the neighborhood, you could eat on credit and submit your salary at month end. Many people working in a train station nearby would eat on credit and submit their meager salary at the end of the month to the woman.

> The woman was very rich. But all her grandchildren became very poor. She had spent their money in advance. The grand children were the collateral for her wealth from the devil.

***

#1. I give thanks to the Lord that there is no human condition that the death of Jesus cannot handle.

Sing "He is Lord, He is Lord. He has risen from the dead, He is Lord. Every knee shall bow, every tongue confess that Jesus Christ is Lord."

#2. By the blood of Jesus, I make a payment for any hidden collateral over my life, over my finances, over my health - in the name of Jesus Christ.

#3. For any satanic creditor making any claim of collateral over my life and the lives of my children, I present the blood of Jesus as a token of my redemption - in the name of Jesus.

#4. In the mighty name of Jesus, I redeem my resources being used to service any spiritual debt.

#5. I redeem any organ of my body being used as collateral for any debt - in the name of Jesus.

The major cry of this woman was for her boys.

#6. I cry unto You, my God, my Father: My children will not suffer whatever their father or mother suffered.

#7. In the name of Jesus Christ, I shall be greater than my parents. I shall be greater than my ancestors.

The New Testament is better than the Old. The glory of the latter house is to be greater than the former. Even Jesus said he that believes in Him shall do greater works than He did on earth (John 14:12). Solomon was greater than David. David only conquered and acquired vast land. But he had no time for any infrastructure. Solomon was a man who built the nation in infrastructure. But his own son, Rehoboam, was a disaster, a spoiler. His father was wise, he was a fool. His father asked for wisdom from God. His son sought counsel from young boys like him. He inherited 12 states and lost 10.

***

#8. I shall be greater than my spiritual fathers. Their limitations shall not be my limitation. I will be an improvement to the last generation.

#9. My children shall be greater than me. They will not suffer what I suffered in life.

#10. Life shall smile on them. They shall find life easier than I have found it.

Prayer Session #5

GIVE ME TRADE SECRETS

*4. And when thou art come in, **thou shalt shut the door upon thee and upon thy sons**, and shalt pour out into all those vessels, and thou shalt set aside that which is full.*

5. So she went from him, and shut the door upon her and upon her sons, who brought the vessels to her; and she poured out.

There is something called Trade Secrets. Elisha instructed the poor woman:

> *"Shut the door upon thee and upon thy sons and pour..."*

It is like saying, don't let people know your trade secrets. It was only the woman and her two sons and Elisha that knew this Board Room Secret.

You might have borrowed vessels from your neighbors, but shut the neighbors out of the secret. Only you and your inner caucus staff should know the secret of this oil.

There are always secrets of success in every endeavor including ministries – I mean secrets that are given by God.

The neighbors of the woman never knew the trade secrets of this oil business. They only discovered this woman had suddenly become an oil merchant.

35

Trade secret is what gives you an advantage over competitors in the same industry or business. Every successful manufacturer has some trade secrets. For example, some nutritionists have told us there is nothing special or any real nutritional value in Coca Cola. But why has it sold billions and billions of bottles since 1886? Even if they write the chemical 'formulae' on the bottle, you may not get the taste even if you get the color. Dr Penberton got a trade secret that has enriched generations financially.

#1. Lord, give me NEW trade secrets; trade secrets that will give me an advantage over others in the same industry, or ministry secrets that will take me beyond this level to make greater impacts in God's kingdom; special grace and anointing that will take my ministry beyond the present level of impact in soul-winning.

The neighbors of this Widow had customers before she started selling oil. They left their former sellers and came to this new oil seller.

#2. Lord, give me a preference in the industry (your specific area of operation). Divert men and women to me.

#3. Lord, give me extra wisdom above others. #4. As you gave Daniel the spirit of excellence among the administrators in Babylon and he became ten times   better than his colleagues, Father, I apply for the spirit of excellence upon my life, my spouse and upon the lives of my children.

***

Joseph left his prison mates in the cell, even some of those he met there. It was his gift that brought him out. He had a gift that unlock secrets.

***

#5. Lord give me a gift that will take me out of my present condition to a new and greater level in life.

#6. I shall not be hidden in the crowds.

#7. From this year, I shall become a wonder and an enigma to my colleagues.

#8. In the name of Jesus Christ, my case shall be different.

***

Praying these prayers very well can bring you to a new level in life and ministry.

Praying these prayers very well can make a major difference in your life and ministry.

Prayer Session #6

I SHALL NOT DIE

AS AN ORDINARY PERSON

2 Kings: 4. 8-17

8. And it fell on a day, that Elisha passed to Shunem, where was a great woman; and she constrained him to eat bread. And so it was, that as often as he passed by, he turned in thither to eat bread.

9. And she said unto her husband, Behold now, I perceive that this is an holy man of God, which passeth by us continually.

10. Let us make a little chamber, I pray thee, on the wall; and let us set for him there a bed, and a table, and a stool, and a candlestick: and it shall be, when he cometh to us, that he shall turn in thither.

11. And it fell on a day, that he came thither, and he turned into the chamber, and lay there.

12. And he said to Gehazi his servant, Call this Shunammite. And when he had called her, she stood before him.

13. And he said unto him, Say now unto her, Behold, thou hast been careful for us with all this care; what is to be done for thee? wouldest thou be spoken for to the king, or to the captain of the host? And she answered, I dwell among mine own people.

14. And he said, What then is to be done for her? And Gehazi answered, Verily she hath no child, and her husband is old.

15. And he said, Call her. And when he had called her, she stood in the door.

16. And he said, About this season, according to the time of life, thou shalt embrace a son. And she said, Nay, my lord, thou man of God, do not lie unto thine handmaid.

17. And the woman conceived, and bare a son at that season that Elisha had said unto her, according to the time of life. -

#1. Ask the Lord to give you inspiration and anointing to pray.

#2. Worship the Lord for some minutes.

"... a certain great woman..."

#3. In the name of Jesus Christ, I will not die an average woman or man. Whatever history will regard as greatness, let it begin to manifest in my life - in the name of Jesus.

#4. Father, I don't need to be looking for great men and women to help me. Make me great also to help lift up others.

#5. Make me great in power, great in substance, great in influence.

Your Word says, "Moses was mighty in words (even as a stutterer) and in deeds." (Acts 7:22). Jesus was great and mighty in words and in deeds. Paul and Apollos were great in speech and in deeds.

#6. Father, make me great in speech and in deeds. Let my words be words of power.

#7. Everywhere I stand to represent You, let my words be filled with Your power - in the name of Jesus.

#8. And Father, any time I stand to speak, let me never misrepresent You in speech or behavior.

#9. Just as Abraham and Sarah entertained some guests that turned out to be people who had answer to their prayers and expectation of over 60 years, Father, bring the man and woman that will be answers to my prayers.

***

Elisha wasn't the first preacher this woman would see. This great woman must have seen men of God before. She could recognize a man of God. But none of them had her miracle. It is not every prophet that has your miracle in his mouth.

***

#10. Father, in the name of Jesus, bring that prophet my way - the prophet that has my miracle in his mouth.

There is a place for prayers and deliverance. But in the case of this woman and the first woman in verses 1-7 Elisha didn't pray. He only made a prophetic declaration. He didn't even say "Thus saith the Lord". He wasn't interested in the reason for the barrenness -whether it was from a demon or natural cause. Whether the cause was a curse, household witches or wizards, he wasn't interested. No deliverance or special healing service.

He didn't have to pray or conduct deliverance. He had a grace upon him that made his words honored by Heaven.

***

#11. Oh my Father, I know there is a place for prayers, deliverance and laying-on of hands, etc. But there is a place for prophetic declaration and authority. Father, give me prophetic unction for solution to human complications.

#12. Lord, make me a solution. Many of Your children are going through pains and hurts. Make me a channel of blessing and solution. Release Your power upon my tongue - in the name of Jesus.

***

Verse 13. *And he said unto him, Say now unto her, Behold, thou hast been careful for us with all this care; what is to be done for thee? wouldest thou be spoken for to the king, or to the captain of the host? And she answered, I dwell among mine own people.*

The woman says in essence, "I don't need any other connection, not even from the President, Prime Minister or Chief of Defense Staff. I am already highly connected. I am already surrounded with great men and women."

If you are the only great or rich person in your extended family or neighborhood or church, you may not enjoy your wealth. The greatness of others does not reduce your own. There is a vastness in God that is capable of making everyone in your family stars. You don't have to be the only star. God filled the universe with trillions and trillions of stars. So, don't pray that only you should be great in the community.

***

41

#13. Father, bless all those who surround me. I pray for every member of my extended family. (Mention them by name). I pray for members of my church who are struggling with financial problems. Father, release the greatness in all of them. Open new doors for them - in the name of Jesus. (Mention some individuals you know).

The woman humbly rejected Elisha's offer of connection.

#14. Lord, take me from this my present level to a level of great satisfaction in life - in the name of Jesus.

> *Verse 14. And he said, What then is to be done for her?*

Elisha insisted he must bless this woman.

#15. Father, from today, let someone receive a divine obligation, divine drive and compulsion to bless me - in the name of Jesus.

***

A few years earlier when there was a famine in the land, God told Elijah, ***"I have commanded the ravens to feed thee"***. When the Brook dried up, God said, *"Go to* ***Zarephat****, I have commanded a widow to sustain thee..."* (1 Kings 17:4, 9).

Ravens are greedy and voracious. But these were the same birds God commanded to bring Elijah's food.

***

#16. Father, command people (even those who are naturally as greedy as ravens) to help me.

#17. Where my Brook has dried up, Command unlikely people to help me - in the name of Jesus.

***

"And Gehazi answered, Verily she hath no child, and her husband is old.

Even a greedy and covetous Gehazi can be used by God to identify my problem and recommend me to my solution carrier!

***

#18. Lord, if you could use Gehazi to help this woman, raise for me some campaign managers to recommend me to my potential benefactors.

***

15 And he said, Call her. And when he had called her, she stood in the door.

16. And he said, About this season, according to the time (calendar) of life, thou shalt embrace a son. ..."

What are you trusting God for by this time next year, or even next month or next week? What are you trusting God to embrace by this time next year - a baby or a spouse? The God of Elisha is still the same yesterday, today and forever. Please, take a good time to pray here.

16 And she said, Nay, my lord, thou man of God, do not lie unto thine handmaid.

17 And the woman conceived, and bare a son at that season that Elisha had said unto her, according to the time of life. -

Even though she didn't express any faith or excitement to receive the miracle prophesied, she received this miracle, nevertheless. That prophetic grace on Elisha cancelled her unbelief.

***

#19. My Father, my Father. By Your love and sovereignty, overrule my unbelief and all my shortcomings - in the name of Jesus Christ my Lord. Let not my unbelief and behavior stop Your miracle in my life - in the name of Jesus.

***

Note: With the inspiration you have received here, please, take a few minutes to make some prophetic declarations and affirmations on your life, your family, ministry and work or business.

Prayer Session #7

LORD, LET THIS BE MY PERIOD OF REWARDS

Thank the Lord God for a new day.

Take a good time to worship His majesty as we enter His presence.

This is the day that the Lord has made. I will rejoice and be glad in it....

2 Kings 4:13.

> *"... Behold, thou hast been careful for us with all this care; what is to be done for thee? wouldest thou be spoken for to the king, or to the captain of the host? ..."*

This woman had been taking care of Elisha and his servant for some time without expecting anything in return. Now it is pay day.

***

#1. Father, let today be my pay day; let this year be my year of rewards - for all my investments of love in people's lives. Let this month be my month of reward. Let this year be the year of my own reward. Whatever love seed I have sown any time, Lord, check my book of records. A day came for the reward of Mordecai for an act of love he sowed. Father, let today be my day. Let archives be checked for my sake.

"....what is to be done for thee? would thou be spoken for to the king, or to the captain of the host? ..."

Here Elisha has assumed a campaign manager for this woman.

***

#2. Lord, raise a campaign manager for me: a man or woman who will speak for me where I cannot speak for myself. You raised a man who spoke for David to give him a job in the Presidency. In any committee or board meeting where a decision will be made about me, speak for me there - in the name of Jesus.

> *17. And the woman conceived, and bare a son at that season that Elisha had said unto her, according to the time of life."*

#3. In the name of Jesus, I will conceive (whatever that means to you. Yours may not be a baby. But you will conceive a miracle.) If you need to conceive an idea that will grow to be a major testimony, receive it now in the name of Jesus!

***

"....and bare a son at that season that Elisha had said unto her, according to the time of life."

***

#4. Father, all the ideas and visions I have conceived for years and have not brought them into reality, this is the month and year of my delivery. I will deliver - in the name of Jesus.

#5. As this woman received her miracle "at that season that Elisha said...", I pray my miracle shall no longer be delayed.

Prayer Session #8

"MY HEAD, MY HEAD"

2 Kings 4:18. 18. "And when the child was grown, it fell on a day, that he went out to his father to the reapers." 19. And he said unto his father, My head, my head. And he said to a lad, Carry him to his mother. 20. And when he had taken him, and brought him to his mother, he sat on her knees till noon, and then died. ------ "And he said unto his father, 'My head, my head'..." That was an attack - a satanic arrow on the child.

#1. Put your right hand on your head and say: My head, my head, you will not be attacked. The head of my children will not be attacked. Their brain will not be attacked. No arrow of the wicked will hit them - in the name of Jesus. (Mention your children by name).

****

Man's life is controlled from his head. Of the five human sense organs, four of these are attached to the head : hearing, seeing, smelling, tasting, smelling. If the head is attacked or infected, the person is finished. If a man's hand or legs are amputated, he can still survive and use other parts. Nick James Vujicic was born with tetra-amelia syndrome, a rare condition characterized by the absence of arms and legs. But Nick became a great pastor, evangelist and motivational speaker. Why, because his brain is still in tact. He is popularly called Pastor Nick. But if the head of a person is attacked, he is gone. That is why the casing for the brain (skull) is very hard. God specially protects the head; but sometimes, it can be damaged.

47

When it is attacked, the person can develop any of the following conditions: Dementia, characterized by loss of memory. Alzheimer's Disease is part of this. There can be brain tumor or cancer and stroke. The part of the brain that is affected determines what happens to the person. Speech, hearing nor sight may be impaired. There can also be the Parkinson's disease characterized by tremor of hands and other parts of the body. There may be cerebral meningitis, epilepsy, some other mental disorders, migraines, sleeplessness, constant headaches, brain infections, brain hemorrhage, etc.

There can also be damages caused by drug abuse. Some of these can be natural, some can also be spiritual attacks on the brain.

None of these will be your portion - in the name of Jesus.

***

Put your hands on your head again and pray:

#2. My head will not be attacked. Lord, I put on the helmet of salvation. I put it on my children and my spouse – in the name of Jesus.

#3. No disease of the brain will come near me.

#4. No arrow will penetrate my head - in the name of Jesus.

#5. I will not suffer brain hemorrhage. I will not suffer stroke – in the name of Jesus Christ.

#6. I will not suffer Parkinson's disease. It is Parkinson's disease, not mine. I am not Parkinson. I am not Alzheimer, so Alzheimer's disease is not my disease.

***

20. And when he had taken him, and brought him to his mother, he sat on her knees till noon, and then died.

The boy sat on the mother's knees. And when it was NOON exactly, he died! It wasn't *after* noon or *before* noon. It was NOON. All Bible translations capture this time. Even the Yoruba translation captures the time of the boy's death as *"ojo-kan-ri"*. It means a time when the sun is directly on the head of a person on earth. It is a time when the two hands of a clock are pointing directly to the sky. That was exactly when the boy died.

I believe it was a timed and programed death. It was as if a spiritual arrow of death was shot at the boy around 10am. The thing was going around the body. By exactly 12 noon, the spirit of death hit the heart. And he was dead.

There are people who are already hit with the arrow of death, waiting for the day of maturity. The day of maturity may not be the same day of the attack. It can be an installmental death.

#7. Any programed death for me or my children will fail - in the mighty name of Jesus.

#8. Any arrow or seed of death already in my body, waiting for a maturity day, my body is the temple of the Holy Spirit. I command you to get out of my body now – in the name of Jesus!

#9. You, my body, you must not harbor anything that does not add value to your life.

***

When David says, **"the sun will not smite thee by day nor the moon by night"**, he meant the sun can smite, and the moon can smite and such smiting could be tragic. David was not talking about just physical sun or moon beating a person. There are certain astral powers and enchantments that occult people can project or program into the sun or the moon to smite a person or an institution. There are people who come under certain misfortunes or attacks or sicknesses during the full moon. Certain afflictions are also activated when some people come under the sun. Some women suffer regular miscarriages at the full moon. Once they come under the moon their body reacts to the program and the baby in the womb is evicted from the body.

***

#10. In the name of Jesus, I will not suffer any satanic stroke from the sun or any astral power.

#11. The sun will not smite my children. The moon will not smite them by night.

#12. My spouse and children will not be smitten by any type of astral forces – in the name of Jesus.

(If the smiting of the boy had been from the moon (lunar power), that boy may have become lunatic or insane for the rest of his life.

#13. None of my children shall be a psychiatric project – in the name of Jesus.

#14. I secure my brain and the brains of my spouse and children by the power of the Holy Ghost - in the name of Jesus.

#15. My children will not be exposed to drugs - in the name of Jesus. Let their minds rebel against any form of drug abuse.

#16. I insulate the brains of my children from satanic seeds and arrows of unbelief and rebellion against God.

#17. My brain is secure - in the name of Jesus Christ. I will not suffer depression or any form of mental breakdown.

#18. I receive strength for my brain. I receive greater cerebral capability for myself and my children. I apply for greater memory activation.

There can be a strange spiritual aura on the head. There are some people who receive incisions on the head or other parts of the body for spiritual 'protection' or one thing or the other. Such heads may reject blessing or favor. Sometimes, when something is wrong with the heart, the head will reject blessing. When Eliab, the first some of Jesse came out to be anointed as king of Israel, Samuel about to anoint him when God restrained him: "I have refused him." God said, He looked at the heart to determine what the head is qualified to receive.

#19. In the name of Jesus, my head will not reject blessing.

#20. Lord, whatever is wrong with my heart that may disqualify my head from favor, cleanse me today by the blood of Jesus Christ.

***

Some heads are carrying strange aura through some strange 'anointing' they have received from certain preachers using some occult powers. Today, there are various kinds of 'anointing oil' people are carrying about.

Some people have received laying-on of hands by people with occult rings or demonic 'anointing'.

51

***

#21. In the name of Jesus, I plead the blood of Jesus Christ on my head. I receive a cleansing of head from all negative aura and strange attachments on my head.

***

There are some people whose hair has been cut in a dream. Some hairs are not cut but simply disappear. I saw a baby in Europe whose hairs disappeared in a night. No strand of hair was left on the head by the morning. The head was shining. And none of the hairs was on the bed. They all simply disappeared in a night. I was naturally frightened when I saw the baby's head!

There are some hairdressers who take women's hairs for rituals. In some religions, a new baby's hairs are shaved and some taken away by the priest to do something with the hair. Such babies already have part of their lives under control.

***

#22. In the name of Jesus, I recover any part of my life or hair that might have been taken by anyone whether in a dream or any way.

#23. Appreciate the Lord for today.

Prayer Session #9

MY MIRACLE WILL NOT DIE

2 Kings: 4: 19.

> *19. And he said unto his father, My head, my head. And he said to a lad, Carry him to his mother.*
>
> **20. And when he had taken him, and brought him to his mother, he sat on her knees till noon, and then died.**

#1. This boy died in his mother's hand. In the name of Jesus, none of my children will die. I will not witness the death of any child.

#2. Whatever God has done in my life will not die. My miracle will not die. No good thing will die in my hand.

#3. No project will die in my hand - in the name of Jesus.

#4. I command every dead project to come alive – in the name of Jesus Christ.

#5. My testimony will not die - in the name of Jesus! Whatever testimony I had before and the enemy has killed it, I call it back to life and manifestation in my hand - in the name of Jesus. Never again will I suffer *failure and loss* (get-and-lose syndrome) in my life - in the name of Jesus.

#6. Whatever I am embracing and smiling about at the moment will not die. My husband will not die. My wife will not die. Any good relationship God has given me will not die.

Prayer Session #10

I SHALL NOT BE IRRESPONSIBLE

"Carry him to his mother"

2 Kings: 4: 19.

> *19. And he said unto his father, My head, my head. And he (father) said to a lad,* **Carry him to his mother.**

The father of the boy was irresponsible. He never made any attempt to pray for the boy or attempt any First Aid. No effort. He simply told his servant, "Carry him to his mother" and he continued his work. This tragedy happened at the time of harvest and the man was in the farm busy with "the reapers" - harvesting. He was more preoccupied with his business than in any family affair. Even when he came back home and saw the wife restless and asking the husband to quickly get a driver and a vehicle that "I may RUN to the man of God", the man never suspected anything. And he never asked for the state of the boy! He never suspected anything was wrong. He was insensitive. He only asked the wife, "But today is not Sabbath or festival day; why are you going to see a prophet?" He doesn't believe in going to church or any religious program if it is not a festival day. He goes to church only three times in a /year - Christmas, New Year and Easter! When there is a spiritual attack, it is women we see going from church to church, from camps to prayer houses. Some of the women are abused and exploited by false preachers while the man is at pop houses drinking and dancing with useless girls or at best busy with the reapers.

#1. I pray for the husbands of our generation who are spiritually irresponsible. You will become responsible.

#2. O God, convert our men! In homes where the women are the priests and spiritual heads, let there be conversion of the men. (Mention any of such husbands you know and bring them before this altar. Ask the Lord to visit them.)

#3. Drinking houses are springing up everywhere in our cities. The major clients are husbands of certain women. O God, arise and convict such men - in the name of Jesus. Let their body systems begin to rebel against those drinks.

#4. Convert our men who spend six hours in pop or club houses but cannot stand to pray for 30 minutes intelligently. In the day of trouble, it is the woman that runs around. O God arise, and give us real men, real husbands, real fathers and real spiritual leaders in the homes.

#5. Give us men of power, men of spiritual authority, men of prayer valor.

Prayer Session #11

I SHALL NOT BE RESTLESS THIS YEAR

2 Kings: 4. 22.

> *And she called unto her husband, and said, Send me, I pray thee, one of the young men, and one of the asses,* **that I may run to the man of God,** *and come again.*

#1. This year I will not see any travail or restlessness over any of my children. I shall not have a cause to be running helter-skelter over any of my children or husband/wife. (Mention your children by name and prophesy on them one by one in this respect.)

#2. Trouble will not visit me. There shall be no evil emergency in my home - in the name of Jesus!

#3. In the day of trouble, I shall not be stranded. In the day of trouble, let there be enough grace to handle any situation. I shall not be helpless - in the name of Jesus.

Jesus said, "Come unto me all ye that labor and are heavy laden and I will give you REST..." (Matt 11:28).

#4. In the name of Jesus, I enter my rest – in my marriage, rest in my business, rest in my body, my health, rest in my brain, rest in my work. I pray for sufficient anointing to handle any domestic emergency.

Prayer Session #12

I APPLY FOR MORE GRACE FOR SOLUTION

2 Kings: 4. 29.

29. Then he said to Gehazi, Gird up thy loins, and take my staff in thine hand, and go thy way: if thou meet any man, salute him not; and if any salute thee, answer him not again: and lay my staff upon the face of the child.

30. And the mother of the child said, As the LORD liveth, and as thy soul liveth, I will not leave thee. And he arose, and followed her.

31. And Gehazi passed on before them, and laid the staff upon the face of the child; but there was neither voice, nor hearing. Wherefore he went again to meet him, and told him, saying, The child is not awaked.

#1. I thank you, Father, I will not have any emergency this week, this month or this year. I thank You, Lord, that this month is not sweeping me away. As I have survived other months, I will see the end of the year in perfect health. My spouse and all my children shall see the end of this year - in the name of Jesus.

#2. As I am entering a new day, new doors will open for me. Every opportunity I ever missed, I bring them forward into the new day.

#3. Father, I apply for the blessings and grace and miracles of the day and month.

#4. In the name of Jesus, I abort the evil pregnancies of this day, this month and this year. I abort such pregnancies over my life, my family and over my nation.

#5. Today, I pray to represent the voice of the church of God in this country: I abort the evil pregnancies for this nation.

#6. I silence every voice of violence and voice of war in this land. Never again shall we experience another war or terror attacks.

#7. All the nations that are waiting to start selling weapons to different ethnic nationalities to execute a civil war by killing themselves - shall wait in vain. They shall be disappointed - in the name of Jesus.

***

Gehazi was given a stick, and some formulas of raising the dead. He faithfully followed all the prophetic instructions and prescriptions of Elisha, but all these didn't solve the problem on ground. Nothing was wrong with the stick or the prescription. But none of these worked. Maybe something was wrong with Gehazi, the minister.

***

#8. Father, I bring myself before you this moment, draw my attention to whatever is wrong with me.

#9. Remove from my life whatever may be hindering the full manifestation of Your power in my life.

***

Today, we rely on many formulas of getting miracles and most of them are not working. Most people are carrying about special bottles of olive oil. Sometimes, different bottles for different problems. In fact, olive oil has suddenly become a big industry in the past 3 decades or so. We carry about 'mantles' and other objects as formulas of miracles.

Yet we are not seeing much result. Jesus carried none of such. He carried grace - grace that was sufficient to deal with any sickness or complications.

> *How God anointed Jesus of Nazareth with the Holy Ghost and with power: who went about doing good, and healing all that were oppressed of the devil; **for God was with him.** (Acts 10:38).*

***

#10. Father, I apply for this grace - the grace for solution. The grace to heal the sick, grace to raise the dead and bring to life destinies that have been killed.

***

Gehazi was empty but carrying an anointed stick. The stick didn't work.

***

#11. Lord, fill my emptiness. I will not be stranded in ministry.

#12. Anoint me with fresh invisible oil.

> *31. And Gehazi passed on before them, and laid the staff upon the face of the child; but there was neither voice, nor hearing. Wherefore he went again to meet him, and told him, saying, The child is not awaked. (Verse 31).*

#13. In the name of Jesus Christ of Nazareth, I will not fail in any ministration again. Every dead situation will respond to my ministrations.

#14. Father, I apply for the anointing to raise the dead. I apply for the anointing to heal the sick.

#15. Many men and women are looking for prophets - any prophet who can solve their problems. Lord, make me a genuine solution.

#16. Release more of your power upon me this day.

#17. Father, begin to disgrace the Gehazis among preachers - covetous men who are exploiting the problems of people to deceive them to collect their money.

***

(The major prayer here is for anointing to be a solution. Take some time after today to pray it again. Examine your motives also. Gehazi probably wanted glory. He ran ahead of Elisha and the woman to go and display power with the stick. But nothing happened. God didn't honor him. He came back frustrated. Judge your motives for seeking anointing.)

Prayer Session #13

DELIVERANCE

FROM DEARTH AND DEATH

2 Kings: 4. 38-40.

> 38. And Elisha came again to Gilgal: and there was a **dearth** in the land; and the sons of the prophets were sitting before him: and he said unto his servant, Set on the great pot, and seethe pottage for the sons of the prophets.

> 39. And one went out into the field to gather herbs, and found a wild vine, and gathered thereof wild gourds his lap full, and came and shred them into the pot of pottage: for they knew them not.

> 40. So they poured out for the men to eat. And it came to pass, as they were eating of the pottage, that they cried out, and said, O thou man of God, *there is death in the pot*. And they could not eat thereof.

Gilgal was supposed to be a place of a new beginning; a place where Israel had a Passover after 40 years of roaming about in the wilderness, a place where a new generation was circumcised, a place where people tasted the "corn of the land" for the first time, a place where Israel began to enjoy the benefits and foods of the Promised Land.

But here after several years, there was DEARTH (scarcity of food, famine, starvation) in the land of Gilgal. There was a school of prophets there; all the students there were caught up in this dearth.

#1. In the name of Jesus, my Gilgal will not experience dearth.

2. The Lord is my Shepherd. I shall not be in dearth.

3. Where food or sustenance are flowing for me at the moment or in the past will not experience a change of condition.

4. My present source of supply shall not dry up. My brook will not dry up – in the name of Jesus.

Gilgal was the place where Manna of 40 years ceased for the children of Israel and they began to eat *the corn of the land*.

> *"And the manna ceased on the morrow after they had eaten of the old corn of the land; neither had the children of Israel manna anymore; but they did eat of the fruit of the land of Canaan that year." (Joshua: 5. 12).*

If your Manna has stopped, look up for the corn of the land. Manna was good; it was supernatural; but it was a daily bread. Manna was a food you could not save till the following day. If you kept it, it would develop maggots. That job or business you have that is able to give you just your daily bread and pay utility bills, is what is classified as Manna. You cannot save from it. It is a wilderness income and sustenance.

5. Father, deliver me from Manna. (Warning! That is a dangerous prayer. You may lose your present job if God answers that prayer! But that is, if the job is only giving you daily bread. But if you have the faith and want to move forward, pray the prayer again.)

6. Father, I will no longer be living on Manna.

7. Take me out of this wilderness sustenance.

8. From this day, I will begin to eat the real corn of this land.

9. My children will not live on Manna.

10. Father, give me a new job or business that will give me access to the real corn of this land. (Every nation has its own 'corn').

Because of this famine in Gilgal, one of the prophets went to look for something he could cook. Eventually, it was poison he cooked unknowingly.

There is dearth in our land today. Where there is dearth, there are deaths. Some of us may not be eating good and healthy foods. The 100 sons of prophets ate death but were delivered.

11. Father, in the name of Jesus, let every poison I might have eaten for years be neutralized in my body.

12. If there is any gradual damage going on in any organ of my body, Father, let Your mercy reverse it – in the name of Jesus.

13. Where I have eaten a pottage of death in the dream, Father, neutralize it and flush out all satanic poisons from my body.

14. I speak to my body to reject every pottage of gradual death I have eaten in dream – in the name of Jesus.

15. By urination, sweating and defecation, my body must reject all the evils I have eaten in dream.

16. Father, rejuvenate my life and lengthen my days.

17. I will not break down in health. No organ or system of my body shall break down - in the name of Jesus.

18. (Pray for anyone you know that may be experiencing severe needs or any sickness.)

Prayer Session #14

THE MAN FROM BAAL-SHALISHA

2 Kings: 4. 42-44.

42. And there came a man from Baal-shalisha, and brought the man of God bread of the firstfruits, twenty loaves of barley, and full ears of corn in the husk thereof. And he said, Give unto the people, that they may eat.

43. And his servant said, 'What, should I set this before an hundred men?' He said again, 'Give the people, that they may eat: for thus saith the LORD, They shall eat, and shall leave thereof.'

44. So he set it before them, and they did eat, and left thereof, according to the word of the LORD.

Even though Elisha neutralized the poison in the pottage and the sons of prophet ate, that miracle could only solve an immediate hunger problem. The miracle did not solve the continued starvation problem of these ministers in Gilgal. No one knew where the next meal would come from. They couldn't go back to the bush to be looking for wild gourds. The last they had almost sent them to the graves.

Nothing was in any farms; no fruit or vegetable in the forest. Food was scarce in Gilgal. But food was available somewhere else - Baal-Shalisha. They cannot go and beg.

There is scarcely anything we need that is not available somewhere and in the hand of someone. Baal-Shalisha was just a few kilometers away from Gilgal. But there was food there. Fruits and grains were growing there. But Gilgal was in dearth.

Your Baal-Shalisha may be next door, next street, next town or far away overseas.

#1. Father, wherever is the answer to my prayer, bring the answer to me.

#2. Whoever has my need in hand, let him locate me.

The man from Baal-Shalisha is unnamed.

#3. The people I don't know will bless me this year.

#4. Strangers I have never met before will be directed to me as benefactors - in the name of Jesus.

The woman who built a guest chalet for Elisha was unnamed.

#5. My life will attract blessings from strangers - in the name of Jesus.

Saul son of Kish had roamed about in villages and forests for three days, hungry and tired. He even passed through Baal-Shalisha looking for his father's asses, but didn't find them there. (1 Samuel 9:4). But immediately he was anointed by Samuel, his life began to attract gifts.

In 1 Samuel: 10. 3-4, Samuel told Saul:

> *"Then shalt thou go on forward from thence, ... and there shall meet thee three men going up to God to Bethel, one carrying three kids, and another carrying three loaves of bread, and another carrying a bottle of wine:*

4. And they will salute thee, and give thee two loaves of bread; which thou shalt receive of their hands."

The men were taking the gifts to God in the church in Bethel. But when they saw Saul with an invisible oil of God upon his life, they diverted two of the three loaves to Saul. It's like saying, 'we see God with you. If we give to you, it is God we have given.'

They didn't know Saul and he didn't know them. These three men were unnamed also. So, my benefactor doesn't have to be a known person.

#6. In the name of Jesus, Something invisible upon my life will begin to attract gifts this year. Gifts shall be diverted to me by the reason of the anointing.

The man from Baal-Shalisha brought bread from his firstfruits.

#7. Father, send to me the man or woman who has my bread in his hand.

The man from Baal-Shalisha gave firstfruits: that is, he saw the gift as a priority above his own needs.

#8. Send me men and woman who will see me as a priority beneficiary for a blessing. Wherever a request of mine is waiting on pending or being delayed for approval, it shall be treated as a priority from this day. Where my file has been kept away for much later date, it shall be brought forth on priority tray - in the name of Jesus.

#9. Father, at this period of the year, begin to speak to my benefactors.

#10. Elisha did not solicit for bread or gift. This year, I will not solicit for gift in any way. All those who have what I need will hear the voice of the Lord.

#11. Father, make me also a blessing to some people this year.

#12. Bless me to be a blessing to some families this period.

#13. I want to be an answer to some people's prayers this season.

Even though the gifts were not brought to the student prophets but personally to the Senior Pastor Elisha, the Prophet didn't eat the gifts alone. He said, "Give unto the people that they might eat...."

Because of famine or dearth in Gilgal, Elisha could have decided to keep the 20 loaves of bread in the fridge and be eating them one or two loaves per day. That would have lasted him some two weeks. But he probably preferred to go on fasting and give the food to members of the congregation or his junior ministers who were starving. There were 100 people in great need. The bread won't be sufficient for them.

> *43. And his servant said, 'What, should I set this before an hundred men?' He said again, 'Give the people, that they may eat: for thus saith the LORD, They shall eat, and shall leave thereof.'*

We have a satirical song in South West Nigeria that expresses a selfish philosophy of some people: "*Bamubamu l'a yo 2x; awa o mo p'ebi npa omo enikankan. Bamubamu l'a yo....* It means, "We are more than satiated 2x; and we don't care if anyone is starving around."

We have leaders stacking millions in different accounts in and outside the country while the people are starving and some picking food from refuse dumps to eat. Unfortunately, we have some church leaders too who pride in their opulence as a sign of their 'faith' and 'anointing' while the sons of the prophet are living in poverty.

#14. Lord, as Your children who have shut our bowels of mercy to the needy people around us, we repent of our wickedness.

Today, our messages are being despised by sinners because they feel we are preaching to them mainly to get what they have and add to our own.

We invoke Malachi 3:8-11 as a curse to the people for not bringing in tithes and offerings to the "store house", so that there might be "meat in My house". The people bring the tithes and offerings but see no meat in the house of God. The sons of prophet (Levites) still hunger, "the stranger, the fatherless, and the widow" (Deut 26:12) who are also supposed to have the meat in the house still starve. Because of these problems, people are reviewing the Tithe doctrine and our "store house" theology.

15. Lord, we have been misrepresenting Your Person and what You came and suffered for. Have mercy on us and give us a new heart.

16. As a nation, give us a new orientation of altruism.

17. Father, give us selfless leaders in politics and in church.

18. All the thieves and oppressors of our land shall be exposed and disgraced.

19. All those who have fattened themselves on our common patrimony, they shall vomit them.

20. Begin to make some prophetic declarations concerning your family and your nation. Cover your family.

Worship the Lord with thanksgiving and praise.

You don't have to pray these prayers only once. If you feel inspired to take them up any other time, please do.

Prayer Session 15

THE MIRACLES AROUND THE BIRTH OF JESUS

Luke chapters 1-2 and Matthew chapters 1-2.

The story around the period of the birth of Jesus Christ is a story of certain impossibilities that God made possible. It starts with a couple "striken in years" who naturally could no longer have a child and who eventually gave birth to a boy.

#1. I thank God for keeping me to this stage of my life. I have passed through the valley of the shadow of death, but You have been with me. Your rod and Your staff have comforted me. I appreciate You for Your ever- presence with me.

#2. Father, as Your mercy endures forever, let not this mercy of protection and preservation expire in my life. Keep me and my family throughout this year - in the name of Jesus.

#3. Lord, whatever people believe is no longer possible in my life (like the case of Zechariah and his wife), do it to my own amazement.

#3. (Please, pray for three specific couples you know that are waiting for the miracle of childbearing).

Angel Gabriel told Zechariah, "Your prayer has been answered; your wife will conceive..." But the man was not praying about having a baby. He was praying (in form of sacrifices) for the nation. He had long stopped praying for babies after about 50 years of prayers and nothing happened!

#4. In the name of Jesus, Father, go to my archive of prayers. The issues I have forgotten about, the problems I have accepted as part of my destiny, Father, revisit them this year.

Zechariah didn't believe the Angel, but Heaven had already released the miracle and the Angel refused to take the miracle back to heaven.

#5. Father, In the name of Jesus, impose a miracle upon me. Enforce Your will and purpose in my life as I go through this year.

Zechariah misbehaved and expressed unbelief even as an old man of God of many years of experience. The Angel punished him but still released the miracle.

#6. O God, whatever it will take you, enforce and impose a miracle upon me this year - in the name of Jesus.

When Zechariah expressed unbelief which normally should have disqualified him, the Angel said, "I am Gabriel, that stand in the presence of God; and I AM SENT... thou shall be dumb and not be able to speak (maybe so he won't spread his unbelief to his wife and others) until the day that these things shall be performed" (Luke 1:19-20).

The Angel said, "I am sent." It is like, "I have an order to deliver this and I can't go back to heaven and give excuses." When God really SENDS a helper to you - your miracle bearer - he will ignore your misbehavior.

#7. Lord, Send me a benefactor that will not give up on me.

The same Angel went to Mary six months later and brought another message of natural impossibility - a virgin to conceive a baby. Mary said, "How Can this be?" When God says He is going to do something, you don't say, "How?"

#8. This year, I will receive divine messengers.

#9. The three people in these passages (Zechariah, Elizabeth and Mary) received miracles they were not expecting. Mary was not praying for a baby. She was praying that her wedding later in the year would be a success; that God would provide resources, wedding gown, cake, etc; that Joseph won't change his mind at the last hour, etc! But the Angel brought a strange miracle she was not praying for.

#10. In the name of Jesus, Father, amaze me this year with a major miracle beyond what I have been praying for and expecting. #

Luke 1:24-25. Elizabeth conceived and hid herself 5 months, most likely the last 5 months of the pregnancy. When her tummy protruded, she felt embarrassed. Neighbors would start gossiping about her. They would say it is an advanced case of multiple fibroids or some abdominal cancer or liver or kidney problems. Most people won't ask her what was wrong. They would conclude she needed to be pitied. So, she hid herself until the baby was born. The baby silenced any speculation.

#11. Father, give me a miracle I cannot hide for too long, a miracle that people will soon see without my announcement, a miracle that will generate speculations and ultimately silence gossips.

#12. Lord, give me an embarrassing miracle this year.

When the miracle of the baby became known to everybody, Elizabeth said, *"Thus has the Lord dealt with me in the days wherein **he looked on me**, to take away my reproach among men."*

#13. O my Father, look on me! Whatever is my reproach among my colleagues, my former classmates, my neighbors, take it away from me this year - in the name of Jesus.

#14. Bless the Lord in worship.

LET WISE MEN ARISE AGAIN
IN THE EAST

Matthew: 2:1-2

> *1. Now when Jesus was born in Bethlehem of Judaea in the days of Herod the king, behold, there came wise men from the east to Jerusalem,*

> *2. Saying, Where is he that is born King of the Jews? for we have seen his star in the east, and are come to worship him.*

#1. I come before You this day to worship You, King Jesus.

#2. I apply for the grace that will carry me throughout this year.

Wise men came from the East to seek for the baby Jesus. Tradition says the men came from Persia, present Iran. They were the religious elite of Persia and probably of royalty.

#3. Father, I pray for Iran. Let wise men rise up again in Iran to seek for Jesus. Let there be a revival of the worship of Jesus in Iran.

#4. Let all Iranians and all people who have travelled from the Middle and Far East and all Muslim lands begin to find Jesus in all the places they are. Many are in Europe, North America and Australia as refugees, business people and students.

Father, let them find Jesus instead of exporting terrorism and rape.#

#5. Let Iran and the whole of Arab world begin to seek for Jesus.

#6. O Jesus, Let them find You in dreams and other supernatural encounters. Let them find You on the internet and public media.

The wise men said, *"We have seen his star in the East and we have come to worship him."*

#7. O Star of Jesus, appear again in the whole of the Middle East, the Gulf region and the whole Islamic world.

#8. Stir up the hearts of Iranians to begin to rebel against the repressive regimes that would not allow them to seek for Jesus and worship him.

#9. Let the power of Islam be broken over Iran and the Arab world. Let the veil of deception of Islam be torn to pieces – in the name of Jesus Christ.

#10. The women in Iran and Arab world are covered in black veils. O God, arise, and let the veils be torn to pieces and burnt away from their hearts. In the name of Jesus, we tear all spiritual veils that cover their minds.

#11. Deliver the wise men and women of the Arab world. Let the learned men begin to see Jesus beyond what they know at the moment.

#12. O God, let this year see unprecedented conversions in the Muslim world.

#13. In 1979, there was an Islamic Revolution in Iran and Ayatollah forced Islam on all Iranians. O God, bring a counter revolution that will overthrow this evil system. Let there be massive rebellion against this oppression and repression in Iran and the Islamic world – in the name of Jesus.

#14. This year, we want to begin to hear good news of liberation from Iran.

#15. As the star of Jesus was seen in a far country, so, Father, I ask that this year, my star, my work, my gift, my product, my value, my ministry be seen from far and near.

#16. My star, my expertise, my gifts will attract men from nations. As wise men came from a far country to seek Jesus, I shall be sought for this year.

Prayer Session #17

DIVINE DIRECTION, INSTRUCTIONS AND EXPERIENCES

Matthew 2:13

> *And when they were departed, behold, the angel of the Lord appeareth to Joseph in a dream, saying, Arise, and take the young child and his mother, and flee into Egypt, and be thou there until I bring thee word: for Herod will seek the young child to destroy him.*

The story surrounding the birth of Jesus Christ is a story full of divine experiences and instructions. If there is any major thing we should pray about in a New Year, it is to have divine encounters for direction.

In the whole Old Testament period spanning thousands of years, there are only a few recorded appearances of angels. But there are several appearances and operations of angels around the time of the birth of Jesus - within about 2 years.

1. Angel appeared to Zechariah.

2. Angel appeared to Mary to inform her of what God wanted to do in her life.

3. Angel appeared to Joseph to instruct him to accept what God has done.

4. Angel appeared again to Joseph to instruct him to run away and relocate to another country.

5. Angel appeared to the Wise Men to ignore Herod and take another road back to their country after seeing Jesus.

6. Angel appeared to Joseph again instructing him to leave Africa and return to his country.

7. Angel warned Joseph not to stay in his town in Judea but to relocate to Nazareth to preserve the life of his boy.

Can we just imagine any of these people taking a decision without these definite instructions? Definite divine instructions are very crucial. If you have a leading that you are not clear about, you won't know what definite action to take and this can lead to a possibility of taking a wrong action.

#1. I praise You, Lord, for Your personal interest in my life and Your interest in the affairs of man on earth.

#2. Father, be personally involved in my life this year.

#3. Do not leave me alone this year to my personal whims and caprices.

#4. Give me divine encounters this year. Father, give me divine experiences of Your presence and power that I never had before.

None of the dreams and experiences here was vague, needing any special interpretation. Sometimes we don't remember our dreams even when they are significant.

#5. This year, Holy Spirit, give me clear dreams, clear revelations, clear instructions.

#6. I will not be foolish. I will not take foolish decisions that will lead to failure, frustrations or any trouble.

#7. I will not take decisions or take a wrong step that will endanger my life or the life of any of my children or relatives.

#8. I will not walk in darkness, but shall walk in the light of Your instructions.

Imagine the Wise Men not hearing God clearly and going back to King Herod to honor him and give him a report and the home address where the baby Jesus was as they had agreed to do. That would have endangered the life of Jesus and the history of the world would have been different.

Imagine that Joseph didn't remember the dream he had or did not understand it that he had to leave his country immediately. That would have endangered the life of Jesus.

Many people have taken decisions or delayed to take certain decisions or actions that have either led them to an early grave or put other people in serious trouble.

The angel said, "Go to Egypt." The instruction was specific - where to go and the urgency of the instruction.

#9. Lord give me the privilege of specific instructions this year.

Just before God told Joseph to relocate to Africa, he had sent the Wise Men to bring gold from a far country. Gold is international currency. It can be exchanged for any currency of any country. So, God provided the forex for the journey and for their stay in a foreign land.

If you go to a country that God did not send you, you bear your own expenses for the trip and you may be doing menial jobs in a foreign land to survive.

Joseph didn't have to do carpentry work to survive in Egypt. He may have been required to register and meet all requirements to work in a foreign land as a non-citizen. But he already had gold.

If already you are in a place His Spirit did not send you, pray, "God, have mercy on me."

When it was time for Joseph to leave Africa, God instructed. Jesus would have grown up in exile.

The longer Herod lived, the longer Jesus would have stayed in Africa as a refugee.

#10. In the name of Jesus, I will not die in any form of exile.

#11. Every Herod over my destiny, over my family, over my community, over my nation, who wants to continue to use his authority to keep me in lifelong destiny exile, let God clear him out of the way.

DEALING WITH HEROD

Matthew 2:16:

> *Then Herod, when he saw that he was mocked of the wise men, was exceeding wroth, and sent forth, and slew <u>all the children</u> that were in Bethlehem, and in all the coasts thereof, from two years old and under, according to the time which he had diligently enquired of the wise men.*

When we do not take some time to meditate on specific scenarios in the Bible, we miss the import of such passages. Imagine in a small city of about 10,000 people with all the surrounding villages, a ruler commanded some military men to enter every house and locate every baby of two years and below (maybe around 100 babies in number) and slaughter all of them – just because he wanted to eliminate one particular baby he could not identify – a baby he saw as a threat to his political dynasty.

Joseph and Mary did not offend Herod. They were not politicians. The Baby Jesus did not offend Herod. Jesus had not started preaching. He had not even started talking. What then was His offence?

He was perceived as a threat to the political career of a ruler. The man was already ruling as King but wanted to continue till death and wanted his children or cronies to take over power and rule perpetually. Before Jesus would grow up to think about becoming a king in Palestine, Herod would have died. But Herod still saw Him as a threat.

Most politicians are concerned and sometimes afraid of whoever is going to take over from them after their term expires. Evil rulers want a person who would not probe their administration after they are gone.

In a way,we cannot really say Jesus did not offend King Herod. His offence was that He "was born king" and some ambassadors had started coming from nations to pay homage to Him, bringing hard currencies. (Gold is international currency).

Sometimes you wonder why you should have an enemy. You are gentle and harmless. You are upright; you mean no harm to anyone. You only go about quietly and hurt no one and you believe you should have no enemy. When people talk about having enemies, you wonder what is wrong with them. You think it is because they are from some superstitious African village.

However, if you were "born king" in a certain environment, get ready to either run away or fight a Herod. Satan is too busy to waste his time on any nonentity. Your life attracts enmity because of what the enemy sees you are going to become in life. The devil may not be interested in your past or even your present. He is concerned about "the glory ahead" of you.

The Wise Men asked Herod, *"Where is he that has been born King of the Jews? For we have seen his star in the east, and are come to WORSHIP him."*

They didn't say they came to salute or greet the "born king".' Rather they came to WORSHIP him! When they came to Herod, they didn't worship. You can salute or bow down in respect and honor for a king. But WORHIP belongs to deity. So, these men were saying the new King they came to see was more than a king. He was royalty of humanity combined with deity. That was Christ's offence #2. He was born to be worshipped.

Third, His reputation had started spreading abroad when He had not even started to rule. Herod knew the foreigners did not come empty handed from that far to "worship" the "born king". They had brought some foreign goods and cash. So, this boy had started earning money and international aids when He had not started to reign.

If you don't deal with the spirit of Herod, he may send you into an exile of destiny. When this spirit first came after Jesus, He was still a baby and could not exert His authority. He had to go into exile. Later, when He grew up, a new Herod (with the same spirit of the former) attempted to kill Him before His time. But Jesus told those who brought the classified information: "Forget it. It cannot be.... Go and tell that fox that I will cast out devils today and heal the sick tomorrow and on the third day, I shall finish my job. A prophet cannot perish out of Jerusalem..." (Luke 13:31-35 paraphrased). It's like, "I have grown up. You can't send me into exile again. I won't run away. I will fulfill my days. I will not die one day before my time."

#1. In the name of Jesus, my Herod will fail in his agenda over my life and destiny.

#2. The Herods of my country will fail – in the name of Jesus.

"Then Herod, when he saw that he was mocked of the wise men, was exceeding wroth..."

#3. In the name of Jesus, I will not be a victim of the fury of the wicked.

#4. My children will not be victims of the fury of the wicked.

Those who suffered in Bethlehem (babies and their parents) were not those who mocked the king. The mockers were foreign 'media' (from the East), the foreign diplomats. But it was the locales that suffered.

#5. In the name of Jesus Christ, I will not suffer for what others have done.

Did the wise men actually mock the king? No. But what they did was regarded by Herod as mockery. They only obeyed God's instruction and decided to disobey the king by taking another route to their country. Sometimes in your attempt to obey God, you may end up offending some people or some establishments.

#6. Father, in every way I decide to obey you this year, defend me if someone is offended.

Mary and Joseph wouldn't understand why their new born baby could be a real threat to a ruling politician and why they had to flee their country in a few hours with their new Baby to become refugees in Africa. They never planned that relocation the previous day. But now, they had to move. After the dream, Joseph travelled out of the country before the sun rose in the morning.

#7. Lord, even when I do not have all the facts of your instruction, let me not rationalize any of Your leadings in my life this year.

It is possible some parents in Bethlehem and the surrounding villages might have dreamt faintly about the impending slaughter of the babies in their area. They may have ignored the premonitions or dreams or did not understand them. Then the enemy struck. After weeping, some of them could have said, "And I saw this in a dream..."

#8. Lord, help me not to take Your leadings for granted or disobey You to my destruction.

When Joseph had a dream to run out of the country with the new Baby and mother, it didn't make sense. But he woke up very early in the morning and moved. It is possible he didn't sleep again after that dream. Sometimes, instead of taking immediate action after a bad dream or an instruction, we feel too sleepy to take an action and we mumble a few words in prayer in two minutes and yawn and sleep back, only to enter into trouble later. We even wake up and forget we dreamt.

#9. Lord, lead me clearly this year.

If the dream weren't clear enough, Joseph may still be looking for a prophet to interpret it till the enemy strikes.

#10. Lord, let Your instructions be very clear to me. Sharpen my spiritual sensitivity.

#11. Holy Spirit, repair my spiritual antenna.

#12. Father, if You have to use parables and symbols for me in communicating to me, please, Lord, make them very clear to me.

#13. I don't want to misinterpret Your instruction or leading this year.

#14. Where and when there is danger, Lord, instruct me.

#15. Let me not be at a wrong place at any time. Direct my movements. Let me not travel at a wrong time.

A Chief of Defense Staff in Nigeria was murdered by "unknown" gunmen while coming from his farm. The gun men may not know him. He probably travelled that road at the wrong time. In the name of Jesus, I will not be anywhere at a wrong time.

As "the steps of the righteous are ordered by the Lord", so the Lord shall direct my steps throughout this year.

As a baby at this time, Jesus could not pray for Himself, but He escaped, because God was taking care of Him.

#16. Lord, continue to take care of me as you have been doing.

The children who died in Bethlehem knew nothing of what was going on. The parents who lost their babies had no political ambition and were never a threat to King Herod. But they suffered the madness of this politician.

#17. This year, I will not suffer loss.

#18. My children shall not be victims of the wickedness of our land.

#19. We put a stop to political madness and viciousness in our land.

#20. All those who kidnap or breed and sacrifice babies and adults to achieve their political ambition will be visited by God in His judgment – in the name of Jesus.

Just before Joseph had to travel abroad to Egypt, God already provided international currency (gold) for transport and upkeep in a foreign land for as long as they would stay there.

#21. From now, before any need arises, I apply for advance blessings, advance provisions – in the name of Jesus

If Joseph only had a dream to travel abroad and he had no money, what would he have done so early in morning?

#22. In the name of Jesus, this year, I shall not be stranded financially.

#23. I shall not be running around for help at any time of emergency needs. In the name of Jesus, I receive provisions before the need arises.

Prayer Session #19

I SHALL RETURN

1 Samuel: 17. 55-58.

55. And when Saul saw David go forth against the Philistine, he said unto Abner, the captain of the host, Abner, whose son is this youth? And Abner said, As thy soul liveth, O king, I cannot tell.

56. And the king said, Inquire thou whose son the stripling is.

57. And as David returned from the slaughter of the Philistine, Abner took him, and brought him before Saul with the head of the Philistine in his hand.

58. And Saul said to him, Whose son art thou, thou young man? And David answered, I am the son of thy servant Jesse the Bethlehemite.

David wasn't really a stranger to Saul the King and Abner the Chief of Defense Staff. David had been the Armor Bearer, a kind of Personal Military Assistant of King Saul and also his personal Chaplain in the palace; he was a personal minister who, through his music, ministered deliverance constantly to the king from the spirit of insanity.

But when the war between Philistines and Israel broke out, David lost his two jobs and went back to his village. The King had no time for any personal ministration of palace worship again. And because David was not officially in the Army because he was still a teenager, the King sent him home to his father, back to the village where he was a shepherd (1 Samuel 17:14-15).

When he came to see his elder brothers on the battlefield about two months later, he saw Goliath as the real problem of Israel; he confronted Goliath and slew him. David was carried shoulder high back to the palace.

Now, go back and read that Bible passage above again.

#1. I appreciate You, Father, for this day (or night).

#2. This shall be a new beginning for me and my family.

#3. Where I had lost reputation, I shall regain it hundredfold.

#4. Where I had lost opportunities, God will create greater ones for me this month – in the name of Jesus.

David lost his jobs in the Presidency, but was brought back to the Palace again.

#5. In the name of Jesus, I will return gain.

The king didn't recognize David again - his chaplain, his personal deliverance minister, his armor bearer - just only after two months!

#6. In the name of Jesus, where I have been forgotten, I shall be recalled.

#7. Where they said they didn't want to see my face again, I shall be the new celebrity. (Pray this prayer very well).

Because David wasn't a trained soldier, Abner, the Chief of Defense Staff, sacked David as armor bearer to the King when war broke out. It was like "This is real war; this is no longer a ceremonial job for a teenager or for a musician." Abner needed a veteran Major or Colonel in the Army to replace David to protect the King.

Immediately David was sacked, Abner forgot about him. By the time David killed Goliath, Abner didn't recognize his face again - just within a few months! This is strange.

#8. In the name of Jesus, where I had suffered rejection, I shall be celebrated again.

David had lost two juicy jobs in the Presidency. But after killing Goliath, he was brought back to the palace.

#9. In the name of Jesus, I will go back to my palace.

#10. I regain every good relationship I have lost in life through my carelessness or through a spiritual attack on my life.

#11. David was taken back to the palace because he killed Goliath. In some cases, one might not be able to gain a lost opportunity until a certain Goliath of one's life dies. In the name of Jesus, my Goliath will die this month.

#12. I am going back to the palace.

(Your palace may not be your job. It can be your marriage. If your Goliath doesn't die, your husband or wife may not call you back for reconciliation).

#14. The Goliath that vows his or her life that you won't marry will die!

#15. That was the month of celebration for David. This shall be a month of my celebration.

#16. As David gained national reputation that month, I pray the Lord will begin to announce me this month.

#17. As David was brought to the King to introduce him as the man who has delivered Israel from national disgrace, so from now on, I shall be brought before kings - political kings, kings in the market place, kings in different spheres of life.

#18. Begin to make some prophetic declarations concerning your life and your family for this month or year.

#19. Make declarations for your nation. Make declarations on your community.

#20. Make declarations concerning the children of God in the Islamic world facing extermination - Syria, Iraq, North West Nigeria and all over the world. Declare the Lordship of Jesus over the nations.

Prayer Session #20

WHOSE SON IS THIS?

Start with worship.

Read again 1 Samuel: 17: 55-58.

> *55. And when Saul saw David go forth against the Philistine, he said unto Abner, the captain of the host,* **Abner, Whose son is this youth?** *And Abner said, As thy soul liveth, O king, I cannot tell.*
>
> *56. And the king said, Inquire thou whose son the stripling is.*
>
> *57. And as David returned from the slaughter of the Philistine, Abner took him, and brought him before Saul with the head of the Philistine in his hand.*
>
> *58. And Saul said to him, Whose son art thou, thou young man? And David answered, I am the son of thy servant Jesse the Bethlehemite.*

We see here that the King did not bother to ask for David's name. His father's name is what concerned him.

The glory of killing Goliath is not only for David. That heroic act exalted the family name. The father was at home, not on the physical battle ground. But it was his name that the king wanted to know. Was he the one that killed Goliath? No; but it was his name the King was asking for. Usually, it is one person that exalts a family or disgraces a family name.

#1 In the name of Jesus, I will be the one to bring glory to my family name.

#2 My children's achievements will announce my family name globally.

#3 My children will make outstanding spiritual exploits, academic exploits and exploits in all areas of life - in the name of Jesus. (Take much time to pray these prayers).

> *Now David was the son of that Ephrathite of Bethlehem-judah, whose name was Jesse; and he had eight sons: and the man went among men for an old man in the days of Saul. (1 Samuel: 17. 12).*

The only achievement of David's father was that he had eight sons and was in the old men's club! Nothing more, nothing significant enough to be recorded in his biography - even though he was now close to the grave.

#4. In the name of Jesus, I shall be greater than my father and mother.

#5. All my children shall be greater than me.

#6. My parents' limitations will not be my limitation.

#7. My own limitations will not be my children's limitations - in the name of Jesus.

#8. What I found difficult, they will do with ease.

#9. What King Saul and all the trained soldiers and David's Elder brothers in the army of Israel could not do with all their military equipment, David did with one stone and a sling! In the name of Jesus Christ of Nazareth, the Son of David, that shall be my story. That shall be the story of my children. What the older generations could not achieve with all their sweats, my children and I will achieve them as a fun and as a game.

Jesse was not physically on the war front. But three of his sons were in the Army plus David. He risked the lives of 4 of his 8 sons for the deliverance of his nation. God rewarded him for this sacrifice.

#10. I pray in the name of Jesus, my sacrifice for this nation shall be rewarded.

#11. My children shall enjoy the benefits of the little sacrifices of prayer and fasting I have made for my nation. The land will reward them. Nations will celebrate them - in the name of Jesus.

> *55. And when Saul saw David go forth against the Philistine, he said unto Abner, the captain of the host, "Abner, whose son is **this youth**? ..."*

#12. The Star of David started to shine while he was still a youth. In the name of Jesus, my children shall be early achievers in life.

#13. Their stars will start shining as youths.

> *56. ".... Inquire thou whose son the stripling is..."*

> *58. And Saul said to (David), Whose son art thou, thou young man?*

Note: "...this youth, the stripping, thou young man..."

The other thing that puzzled the King was David's age.

#14 In the name of Jesus, my children shall be a puzzle to their generation. They shall be a wonder. They shall be an enigma to the older generation.

94

#15. All my children shall be early achievers in life - in the name of Jesus.

#16. Of all the eight sons of Jesse, only David was a star. I don't have to be the only star in my family. It is not only one star that is needed among my children. There is a vastness in God that is capable of making all my children stars in different areas of life. The universe is full of trillions of stars. All my children shall be stars – in the name of Jesus Christ.

What if Jesse had died before this achievement of David? Remember it was David's father that King Saul was asking for. What if he had died before then?

#17. I shall be alive on the days of my children's celebrations - in the name of Jesus.

#18. My honor and celebration shall not be done posthumously. No man or woman will represent me in the days of my children's glory - in the name of Jesus.

#19. I will not be bedridden or be in any affliction on the days of my children's glory and celebrations – in the name of Jesus.

Prayer Session #21

O GOD, DELIVER MY DELIVERER!

(Elijah and His Nameless Servant)

1 Kings: 19: 3-4.

> *3. And when he saw that, he arose, and went for his life, and came to Beer-sheba, which belongeth to Judah, and left his servant there.*
>
> *4. But he himself went a day's journey into the wilderness, and came and sat down under a juniper tree: and he requested for himself that he might die; and said, It is enough; now, O LORD, take away my life; for I am not better than my fathers.*

Elijah had only one member in his ministry. When the man of God came under depression because of witchcraft threat and influence of Jezebel on his life, the servant lost his own distinctive ministry. He lost his ministry career in Beersheba. We never heard of him again. God had to replace him. God asked Elijah to go and look for and anoint a farmer, Elisha, to take over the ministry of this servant.

Whatever Elisha became in life as a prophet was what this nameless servant of Elijah could have become.

Sometimes, your prophet may need prophecy too; your deliverer may need deliverance too. When your personal prophet or deliverer has a problem and needs deliverance, and you don't pray for him and you probably join those who are criticizing him, it may affect your own deliverance and destiny.

Sometimes, it may not be you that really needs deliverance. It may be your deliverer that needs a ministration. When he is free you are free. When he is free you enter your destiny. If he is not free, you remain in your problem.

Prayer #1: O Father, in the name of Jesus, deliver my deliverer from every negative influence he or she may be having on his or her life and mind.

(Pray this prayer very well).

DELIVERANCE OF MOSES AND DELIVERANCE OF ISRAEL

While Israelites were suffering extra years of bondage in Egypt, God didn't look for an alternative to Moses. Moses was the destined deliverer of Israel. God preferred that Israel should suffer extra 30 years in Egypt to finding an alternative deliverer to Moses. So long as Moses remained in the wilderness in Midian, over 3 million Israelites would continue to cry, sigh and groan under bondage and hard labor in Egypt.

Strangely, God doesn't always look for an alternative deliverer easily. Even when Moses gave about 11 complaints and excuses why God must send someone else to deliver Israel (Exodus 4), God dismissed all the complaints and refused any other alternative.

Your destined deliverer is not easily replaceable. God may have put all the grace and resources to help you in him. But he may need to be delivered first to be able to deliver you.

If the finances of your destined benefactor are under a siege, it would affect you. If your benefactor is having myriads of problems that take all his attention, he won't remember you.

If your destined spouse is under an attack of delay and frustration, he or she won't look at your direction. He would pretend he doesn't need a wife yet.

#2. O God, today, deliver my deliverer.

#3. Whatever influence there may be on his or her life, finances or health, Father, deliver him/her - in the name of Jesus.

Even though Moses was several hundreds of miles away in the wilderness, God had to locate him to come to the rescue of Israel in Egypt.

#4. Father, locate my deliverer wherever he may be on the planet Earth and deliver him for me. In the name of Jesus, he must not die in that wilderness.

#5. Ask the Lord to send His Angel to deliver all those who have been captured by Islamic terrorists from the hands of their Egyptian captors today.

Worship His Majesty.

Prayer Session #22

BACK TO THE VILLAGE

1 Samuel: 17:15.

15. But David went and returned from Saul to feed his father's sheep at Bethlehem.

This verse shows a serious negative turning point in the history of David. Many of us find ourselves at this point at one time or the other. David already had two plumb jobs in the palace - Personal Military Assistant to the King and personal deliverance minister/chaplain to the king. But when war broke out, the king had no time for any demon. He wanted to face a physical Goliath. (He didn't know that even the physical Goliath was demon possessed and would need a Dividic anointing to deal with). Because David's potentials were underrated, he was sent packing. He lost the two jobs and went back to the farm.

#1. I declare in the name of Jesus that those who have underrated my potentials and ignored me will soon discover their error.

#2. They will soon be looking for me - in the name of Jesus.

David's classmates or fellow farm boys who were already envious of him when he left the farm and got two jobs as personal staff of the King would now be rejoicing in their heart when they saw David back in the village. He was not on holiday or briefly at home for Christmas, but he was actually back to the farm "to feed the father's sheep" as before. Any of his lazy elder brothers who was asked to take over that farm work would now be happy that David was back to the farm.

To go back to the village signifies backwardness in life. It could be loss of job and settling down for a less honoring one. It could be marriage failure etc. Sometimes, some village, community, ancestral or family altars force or call people back to the village, no matter how successful they might have been in the city or even overseas. Some will go back and die as fishermen or peasant farmers in the village. They tell stories of how big and comfortable they were in the city before things changed. That will not be my portion.

#3. Every power waiting to welcome me back to the village life, you will wait in vain.

#4. In the name of Jesus, I will not go back to 'the village' of my destiny.

#5. Every altar calling me back into poverty, fall down and scatter.

#6. In Jesus name, my life will not respond to such an altar.

#7. I disconnect my destiny, my career, my resources, my marriage - from any evil altar - in the name of Jesus!

#8. My status in life will not decrease.

#9. I will not know demotion in status. I will not know spiritual demotion, or financial or social demotion - in the name of Jesus.

Those who had congratulated Jesse for his lucky boy's employment and status in the palace would have gone to sympathize with him when they saw the boy back in the farm.

#10. In the name of Jesus, those who are admiring my present status will not later sympathize with me.

#11. Those who are envious of my present status will not see me back in the village of life.

#12. Those who are envious that I have gone ahead of them will not mock me later.

Some years ago, I preached from this verse in a Friday night vigil in London. By early Saturday morning as soon as she got home, one of the sisters who attended the program was arrested by Immigration officials as an illegal immigrant. I felt very bad when I heard of it. We started praying. By Monday, she was taken to the Airport for deportation – to be back to the village. All arrangements were concluded. She was already at the Departure Hall. She was confused and didn't even know what to pray about because she was guilty.

But suddenly, she said to herself, "How could I be sent back to the village after such a prayer session?"

Instead of feeling helpless and dejected, her faith rose and she said, "No! I refuse to go back to the village in disgrace."

She was still praying and we also were praying for her at home. Suddenly, a fax message came in to the immigration desk at the Airport - that the arrest and deportation process was a mistake! This was fifteen minutes to boarding the plane back to Nigeria in shame!

Unknown to her, her younger brother was already in the aircraft - being deported to Nigeria. The devil had organized that joint disgrace for the family. But she escaped.

#13. In the name of Jesus, I shall not be disgraced. Any arranged shame for my life and family is cancelled - in the name of Jesus.

#14. Any shameful event the enemy thinks he has perfected concerning my life this year is hereby nullified in the name of Jesus.

#15. I shall not be deported from glory to shame.

#16. My glory will not turn to shame.

#17. My laughter shall not turn to weeping.

#18. Whatever I am celebrating at the moment will not turn to sorrow.

#19. Nobody will have a reason to sympathize with me - in the name of Jesus.

#20. My children shall not be demoted in life.

#21. As a married woman, I shall not return to my father's house or my father's name again as my surname. #22. I shall not return to the village by loss of husband or rejection or any matrimonial failure.

Prayer Session #23

MY BENEFACTORS WILL NOT FORGET ME

1 Samuel 16:55-58

> *55. And when Saul saw David go forth against the Philistine, he said unto Abner, the captain of the host, **Abner, whose son is this youth?** And Abner said, As thy soul liveth, O king, I cannot tell.*
>
> *56. And the king said, Inquire thou whose son the stripling is.*
>
> *57. And as David returned from the slaughter of the Philistine, Abner took him, and brought him before Saul with the head of the Philistine in his hand.*
>
> *58. And Saul said to him, Whose son art thou, thou young man? And David answered, I am the son of thy servant Jesse the Bethlehemite.*

This is strange. David was a minister to King Saul. He was a benefactor to Saul. How could Saul so easily forget his benefactor within weeks! Yes, weeks. The war lasted a little over 40 days before David came to the scene (1 Sam 17:16). It was when the war broke out that David lost his jobs in the palace and went back home (1 Samuel 17:15). Saul was a beneficiary of the grace and anointing of God upon David. But the King was also destined to be the benefactor of David. Now, when the time came for him to act as a benefactor to David, he

103

forgot who David was – and so soon! He had to ask Abner who David was. Abner, the Chief of Defense Staff, too did not remember the ADC of the Head of State who had been there about two months ago. David had to introduce himself again to King Saul and Abner.

1) Father, let all those who have forgotten me rise now to my help.

2) All those I once helped and who are now in a position to help me but who have forgotten me or not interested in helping me, Father, touch their hearts - in the name of Jesus.

It was the distraction and overwhelming problems from Goliath and the Philistines army that made Saul to forget his benefactor. Sometimes, a person who should help you is unable to do so because of some personal or family spiritual challenges and wars the person may be facing.

3) Father, I want you to intervene in the case of any challenge that anyone who can help me is facing at the moment. Let his Goliath be disgraced.

Instead of getting angry with the person who should help you, take the next few minutes to pray for him or her. You may not know what he is passing through or what is passing through him.

4) Very soon, I shall be invited for the community or national or international celebration of my children - in the name of Jesus.

Give praise to God.

Prayer Session #24

BACK TO THE PALACE

Now, back in the village, David was sent by his father to see the welfare of his three elder brothers who were facing Goliath. It was then that he was carried shoulder high back to the Palace after he killed Goliath.

1 Samuel: 18. 2.

> *12. And Saul took him that day, and would let him go no more home to his father's house.*

After David killed Goliath and he was brought to the king, the king now realized his earlier mistake of sacking David. He restored him to the palace *"and would let him go no more home to his father's house."*

***

#1. In the name of Jesus, my glory shall be restored.

#2. My present or former disgrace shall be turned to multiple honors - in the name of Jesus.

***

David was known only in the palace and to the palace staff when he was first employed. But after killing Goliath, he became a national hero. The whole nation now knew him. Women composed a song spontaneously to celebrate him.

105

They would have been widows if David had not come to the battleground. The whole of Philistine nation now knew David and feared his name! Nations heard about him, and till today, everybody knows about David and that singular achievement. Many modern movies have been produced to reenact David's achievement.

***

#3. In the name of Jesus, my latter glory shall be greater than my former and the present.

#4. In the name of Jesus, whatever opportunities and dignity I have lost before, I regain them in multiplies.

***

Goliath that was the cause of loss of job for David was also the opportunity for David's lifting.

***

#5. My present Goliath will be the agent of my promotion.

#6. In this nation, I shall soon be celebrated.

#7. My children shall be celebrated. They shall be national heroes wherever they are on earth - in the name of Jesus.

***

Maybe the enemy has always resisted your entrance to any palace.

***

#9. From today, I decree: Every power that is obstructing me from entering the palace of my life, be crushed before me. I bulldoze you out of the way - in the name of Jesus.

***

I don't know the palace you have lost. Ask the Lord to take you back there. Were you deported or demoted? Ask the Lord to take you beyond what you lost. Are you facing a complicated deportation charge? Heaven will intervene. Worship the Lord and give Him praise. He is the same yesterday, today and forever!

Prayer Session #25

FROM LODEBAR TO THE PALACE

Below is the case of a prince who could have died as a poor tenant in a village, but who was brought back to the palace by favor.

2 Samuel: 9:1-14

> *1. And David said, Is there yet any that is left of the house of Saul, that I may shew him kindness for Jonathan's sake?*
>
> *2. And there was of the house of Saul a servant whose name was Ziba. And when they had called him unto David, the king said unto him, Art thou Ziba? And he said, Thy servant is he.*
>
> *3. And the king said, Is there not yet any of the house of Saul, that I may shew the kindness of God unto him? And Ziba said unto the king, 'Jonathan hath yet a son, which is lame on his feet'*
>
> *4. And the king said unto him, Where is he? And Ziba said unto the king, Behold, he is in the house of Machir, the son of Ammiel, in Lo-debar.*

5. Then king David sent, and fetched him out of the house of Machir, the son of Ammiel, from Lo-debar.

6. Now when Mephibosheth, the son of Jonathan, the son of Saul, was come unto David, he fell on his face, and did reverence. And David said, Mephibosheth. And he answered, Behold thy servant!

7. And David said unto him, Fear not: for I will surely shew thee kindness for Jonathan thy father's sake, and will restore thee all the land of Saul thy father; and thou shalt eat bread at my table continually.

8. And he bowed himself, and said, What is thy servant, that thou shouldest look upon such a dead dog as I am?

9. Then the king called to Ziba, Saul's servant, and said unto him, I have given unto thy master's son all that pertained to Saul and to all his house.

10. Thou therefore, and thy sons, and thy servants, shall till the land for him, and thou shalt bring in the fruits, that thy master's son may have food to eat: but Mephibosheth thy master's son shall eat bread always at my table. Now Ziba had fifteen sons and twenty servants.

11. Then said Ziba unto the king, According to all that my lord the king hath commanded his servant, so shall thy servant do. As for Mephibosheth, said the king, he shall eat at my table, as one of the king's sons.

12. And Mephibosheth had a young son, whose name was Micha. And all that dwelt in the house of Ziba were servants unto Mephibosheth.

13. So Mephibosheth dwelt in Jerusalem: for he did eat continually at the king's table; and was lame on both his feet."

These days, we often pray against the effects of evil things our parents or ancestors have done. But our progenitors also did some good things which they may not have waited to enjoy. They may have done some great things that we should tap from. It is time to begin to harvest some great character investments of our fathers.

Mephiboshet's father, Jonathan, was very good to David. But Jonathan died without enjoying the reward of his good deeds.

Now, David was looking for any of his surviving sons for a payback.

***

#1. In the name of Jesus, I will begin to harvest the good investments of my fathers.

#2. The Bible says, *"A good man leaveth an inheritance for his children's children"* (Proverbs 13:22). In the name of Jesus, I tap into the good my father or mother might have done to anyone any time.

#3. Again, the Bible says, "Give and it shall be given unto thee..." Whatever good things my parents have given - in kindness and in cash that were not rewarded either because of their other sins or because of satanic attacks they could not deal with, or because of people's ingratitude or maybe the beneficiaries had no means of repayments, I receive the payments now in good measure, pressed down, shaken together and running over – from different parts of the world.

'Something' suddenly spoke to David's heart, "There is someone you need to bless whom you have not blessed; go and locate him."

***

#5. Father, from this moment, let 'Something' begin to speak to someone about helping me.

#6. No matter how comfortable I may be, Lord, I know there is something in someone's hand that can add more value to my life. Father, begin to speak to such kings for me – in the name of Jesus.

#7. Let those who have what I need whom I cannot go to ask for help begin to develop eagerness to help me.

#8. Let unsolicited help come to me and my children – in the name of Jesus.

***

Mephiboshet was in the village of Lodebar hiding, whereas the man he was hiding from sought for him to bless him. Because his grandfather was a bad man and fought David all his life, he thought David would kill him. It was while he was running away for fear of David that he had an accident and became crippled.

***

#9. In the name of Jesus, I shall be sought for and sought after to be honored, even by those I never expect any good thing from.

***

3. And the king said, Is there not yet any of the house of Saul, that I may shew the kindness of God unto him? And Ziba said unto the king,

111

'Jonathan hath yet a son, which is lame on his feet'

The second information Ziba gave to the king about Mephi wasn't necessary: *"lame on his feet"*. Such a statement may be mischievous. Ziba was happy that Mephi was in Lodebar and he expected him to die there while he, Ziba, continued to enjoy all that Mephi's father and grandfather left behind in the city.

It was like saying, "Are you thinking about helping this man? Do you want to bring him from the village to the palace? Did I hear Your Excellency say you even want him to sit down at the table with you and be eating as one of your sons? Well, before you decide finally, let me tell you something you don't know about this man. He is a disabled man. He cannot travel from the village. He can't drive, he can't even sit well on a horse unless they tie him on the horseback! He can't be useful in the palace. As a crippled man, he is going to be an embarrassment to the palace beauty. People would think he is one of your sons. Do you want foreign diplomats and tourists who visit the palace to see such a person in the palace and at the meal table and think he is one of your children? Think about it."

Ha! Ziba! May God disgrace my Ziba!

***

#10. In the name of Jesus, anyone who wants to spoil me for his own selfish purpose shall be disgraced.

***

Someone is thinking about giving you a job, a contract or promoting you or helping you in any way or marrying you or connecting you with a good business or marriage partner, and he just shared the thought in the presence Ziba. And he said, "Who? Did I hear you mention 'John or Lara Mephis'? You better go and pray very well. I am not saying don't help him; I am not saying don't promote her; I am not saying don't marry her. But if you enter trouble later, don't call me..."

***

#11. In the name of Jesus, my Ziba is silenced permanently.

#12. Every Ziba misrepresenting me before my benefactors, my God will lift me up above you.

#13. My benefactor will ignore my Ziba and call for me.

#14. Ziba, the spoiler, Ziba, the slanderer, the calumniator, the despiser, who is bringing forth my weakness before my benefactors, the Lord will disappoint you - in the name of Jesus!

***

Ziba had taken over the estates and farms and the family business empire of Saul and Jonathan. He was enjoying all these even though he was a servant. He now married more women and had 15 sons and 20 servants. But Mephis, the heir to the estate, was living as a tenant in a village.

***

#15. Every Ziba sitting on my spiritual inheritance, or any of my blessings, my promotion, my marriage, my application, payment of the contract I did, my gratuity, any Ziba sitting on my benefits anywhere, let the Holy Ghost fire unseat you - in the name of Jesus!

***

(Please, pray that last prayer in your own native language)

The King said, Go and bring Mephiboshet from the village, Lodebar. Bring him back to the palace.

#16. In the name of Jesus, my benefactors will ignore my detractors.

#17. In the name of Jesus Christ, I will not die in Lodebar.

#18. I am going back to the palace of my inheritance - in the name of Jesus.

#19. All the Zibas that have eaten my wealth, that have swallowed down my benefits, I command you to vomit them - in the name of Jesus.

#20. All the Zibas who have swallowed down our wealth in this nation, you shall vomit them.

#21. All altars, all treasure houses harboring my inheritance, vomit them - in the name of Jesus.

***

If you can create some time, pray from the book of Job 20:4-29, concerning our personal and national Zibas.

Give praise to God.

Prayer Session #26

LORD, LEAD ME TO THE RESTING PLACE

Numbers: 10: 33.

> *And they departed from the mount of the LORD*
> *three days' journey: and the ark of the covenant*
> *of the LORD went before them in the three days'*
> *journey, TO SEARCH OUT A RESTING PLACE*
> *FOR THEM -*

The journey into a year is more than 3 days journey. The most important thing in this journey is the leading of the Lord. The Ark of Covenant went before the children of Israel "to search a resting place for them."

No GPS or Satellite Navigator can search for you a place of rest for your soul. But there is a Holy Navigator that can navigate our lives properly for the rest of this year.

Financial rest is a place where you won't think about how to pay rent, how to pay the children's tuition fees, how to feed, etc.

A resting place is a place of thanksgiving, a place you get to and make a sigh of relief. It is a place of 'arrival'.

For the bachelor or single woman who has been praying all through the year, the resting place is a place of engagement or marriage.

There are some people who thought their marriage was to be their resting place; but they discovered after a few years they have not really entered into the resting place.

Without changing your marriage, God is searching for you a resting place in that same marriage. The Ark of Covenant has come to your home, in the name of Jesus. In the next few months, the Ark of Covenant will give you direction.

For the business man who has pursued many deals for several months or years that never closed, promises that never materialized, for the family members who had desired to move to their own property before the end of this year, the resting place is the place of testimony. It is a place of spontaneous Hallelujah! It is a place where new songs spring from your spirit.

God will work out something for you.

**

#1. Father, no matter what turbulence, restlessness and disappointments I have experienced in the past, I believe there is a resting place for me in the months ahead. There is a resting place for me this year. Lord, go ahead of me and lead me to the resting place.

#2. I have searched, I have browsed; I have searched from the minds and counsels of men, but they have not brought me to the place of rest. Thou Holy Navigator, I hand over my life for the rest of this year to Your complete control.

#3. Father, lead me to the place I will have rest.

#5. Father, You went ahead and FOUND a resting place for Your people. Human and natural navigation satellite navigator cannot search for a resting place for me. Navigate my life for me.

#6. The Ark searched for a resting place and found it within only 3 days. My journey into my resting place shall not be longer again. I enter my resting place this year - in the name of Jesus.

#7. Because God will navigate my life, I will not enter into trouble this year. I will not travel to a wrong place or at a wrong time.

#8. David said, *"the Lord is my Shepherd, I shall not want, He leadeth me besides the still waters, He restoreth my soul ..."* That is a place of rest. Lord, You are my Shepherd, lead me beside the still waters of health, financial still waters, matrimonial still waters - in the name of Jesus.

#9. Worship the Lord and give Him praise. He is the same yesterday, today and forever! He still navigates the life of His children.

Prayer Session #27

DELIVERANCE FROM
DESTINY MERCHANTS

Genesis: 37: 26-27.

> *26. And Judah said unto his brethren, "What profit is it if we slay our brother, and conceal his blood? Come, and let us sell him to the Ishmaelites, and let not our hand be upon him; for he is our brother and our flesh." And his brethren were content.*

It is not all your enemies that want to kill you. Some of them feel there is no profit killing you. They prefer to see you suffer till you die a natural death. For some, it is better to 'sell' or exchange your glory or destiny. This is particularly common in polygamous homes where there is always a competition among the wives who want their own children to excel and be above others in the family.

***

#1. Worship the Lord.

#2. Father, whatever it is that has been sold out of my life, redeem it in the name of Jesus.

#3. I reverse any spiritual trade-by-barter that has taken place over my destiny or those of my children.

That Scripture says, "Come, and let us sell him to the Ishmaelites, ..."

Ishmaelites are still very much involved in slave trade today. It is not only in Libya that slavery is going on. Individuals are being held as slaves all over the Arab world. Many ladies from Nigeria, Ethiopia, Philippines, India and other parts of the world are serving as sex slaves in the Arab world today.

Destinies of nations too have been sold to the Ishmaelites to get oil.

***

#4. Father, all those who are victims of modern slavery, let Heaven release them.

#5. We redeem the nations whose destinies have been sold to Ishmaelites.

***

The future destiny of Europe is being sold to the Ishmaelites. Let heaven redeem the destiny and future of Europe - in the name of Jesus.

Prayer Session #28

"...THIS IS HE: ... HE IS LIKE HIM: ... I AM HE."

John: 9. 1-9.

1. And as Jesus passed by, he saw a man which was blind from his birth.

2. And his disciples asked him, saying, Master, who did sin, this man, or his parents, that he was born blind?

3. Jesus answered, Neither hath this man sinned, nor his parents: but that the works of God should be made manifest in him.

4. I must work the works of him that sent me, while it is day: the night cometh, when no man can work.

5. As long as I am in the world, I am the light of the world.

6. When he had thus spoken, he spat on the ground, and made clay of the spittle, and he anointed the eyes of the blind man with the clay,

7. And said unto him, Go, wash in the pool of Siloam, (which is by interpretation, Sent.) He went his way therefore, and washed, and came seeing.

8. The neighbors therefore, and they which before had seen him that he was blind, said, Is not this he that sat and begged?

9. Some said, This is he: others said, He is like him: but he said, I am he.

The neighbors of this man observed three things that caused controversy among them. First, they no longer saw the man SITTING where he normally sat. Second, He was no longer BEGGING money from any of them. Third, he was NOW SEEING all of them.

Sitting down can be a state of rest. But it can also be a state of stagnation. The man born blind here was not resting. That spot had become his permanent 'office' address. That was where he was earning money. The neighbors who came expecting to see the man in his normal location, normal address, discovered he was no longer on that spot. That was their first shock.

***

#1. In the name of Jesus, I will not remain in this same location or position in life as I have been throughout this year. (If your present position is the best and highest you can ever be, I praise God for you. But if not, say): Before this time next year, my location would have changed. (This may mean many things to different people - wedding, a new job, change of status that brings a change of office, home or residence, etc. Please take a few minutes to meditate on this to pray it. God has not designed us to be stationary. There are massive movements in the whole universe. The Earth itself is moving; all planets are moving. I cannot remain on the same spot in any area of my life.

#2. Those expecting to see me in my present 'address' by this time next year shall be disappointed; they shall be confused – in the name of Jesus.

***

The second thing that caused confusion for the neighbors that they couldn't recognize the man was that he was not begging any of them for money. It wasn't that he was now suddenly rich. Jesus just healed him. He had not started work to earn money. But he knew that his credentials for begging have been destroyed by the anointing. He felt it would be fraudulent for him to still be begging for alms when he could now see. Moreover, it is not dignifying to be a beggar.

***

#3. Father, any credentials that make me to be a beggar in any form, destroy them by Your anointing - in the name of Jesus.

***

Some neighbors may not give alms because they loved the man or pitied his condition. Some people give alms as a sacrifice or ritual for their own benefits. Sometimes, it may be because they were told by their witchdoctors to give alms to a beggar to transfer their sickness or problem or poverty to the beggar as he collects the money. Such people would be disappointed when the man's eyes are now open and he wasn't interested in their alms again.

***

#4. Father, thank you very much for all those you have used for me to meet my desperate needs in one way or the other at any time, all those I have asked for help and they have honored my request. I appreciate them and I ask that you honor them this year.

#5. I pray that in this year, I shall be the helper and not the one to be helped. Change my status.

***

*"Some said, This is he: others said, He is like
him: but he said, I am he."*

The miracle took place in two verses. But all the remaining 39 verses in that chapter are about the controversy generated by that miracle.

***

#6. Father, do a single miracle in my life that will change the rest of my history forever.

TURNING MY CAPTIVITY

Job: 42. 10.

> *10. And the LORD turned the captivity of Job, when he prayed for his friends: also the LORD gave Job twice as much as he had before.*
>
> *11. Then came there unto him all his brethren, and all his sisters, and all they that had been of his acquaintance before, and did eat bread with him in his house: and they bemoaned him, and comforted him over all the evil that the LORD had brought upon him: every man also gave him a piece of money, and everyone an earring of gold.*
>
> *12. So the LORD blessed the latter end of Job more than his beginning: for he had fourteen thousand sheep, and six thousand camels, and a thousand yoke of oxen, and a thousand she asses."*

"When the Lord Lord turned AGAIN the CAPTIVITY of Job..."

This statement indicates that the losses Job suffered were actually CAPTIVITY. His wealth, business, health, children, reputation, honor were CAPTURED in the spirit realm.

However, when the Lord RETURNED the things that were captured in the spirit, the physical things began to come.

Your money, job, marriage, relationship, contracts, health or things that belong to you can be captured in the spirit. Sometimes when you suffer some losses, it may be they were already captured in the spirit. Everything that made Job great, honorable and respected was taken away by Satan.

***

#1. Whatever has been captured in my life in the spirit, Father, RETURN it - in the name of Jesus Christ.

***

When the captivity of Job was turned again, "all his brethren and his sisters, friends and acquaintances, came" and brought money, gold, cattle, etc.

Where were all the brethren for all the period that Job was suffering?

A man's benefactors can be under captivity - their minds and their own resources. Once the mind of your benefactor is captured, he would change or delay any decision he ever made to help you.

***

#2. Father, release my benefactors. Release their resources; release their minds that are being manipulated.

***

David said in Psalm: 126.

> 1. When the LORD turned <u>again</u> the captivity of Zion, we were like them that dream.

2. Then was our mouth filled with laughter, and our tongue with singing: then said they among the heathen, 'The LORD hath done great things for them.'

***

#3. Father, TURN AGAIN MY CAPTIVITY SUDDENLY.

Satan made a strong case against Job.

#4. Whatever demand the enemy is making over my life, over my finances, over my spouse, my marriage, my children, let it not be granted.

#5. Father, I will not know affliction by experience.

***

Job said, "What I feared has come to me."

Because of age, some people fear that they may never marry again or have children.

You saw some sick people in an hospital and you begin to fear it might be your turn soon. You hear of certain people close to you dying of cancer, etc, and some secret fear begins to well up in you that it may be your own turn soon.

#6. Whatever fear I am having, I will not experience it. My fear will not become a reality in my life - in the name of Jesus.

Prayer Session #30

RETURN MY BLESSING, NOW!

1 Kings: 3. 16-20.

16. *Then came there two women, that were harlots, unto the king, and stood before him.*

17. *And the one woman said, O my lord, I and this woman dwell in one house; and I was delivered of a child with her in the house.*

18. *And it came to pass the third day after that I was delivered, that this woman was delivered also: and we were together; there was no stranger with us in the house, save we two in the house.*

19. *And this woman's child died in the night; because she overlaid it.*

20. *And she arose AT MIDNIGHT, and took my son from beside me, while thine handmaid slept, and laid it in her bosom, and laid her dead child in my bosom.*

Judges: 5:12.

Awake, awake, Deborah: awake, awake, utter a song: arise, Barak, and LEAD THY CAPTIVITY CAPTIVE, thou son of Abinoam.

Destinies are exchanged and blessings are stolen mostly in the NIGHT. Blessings are captured in our lives when we are sleeping.

***

#1. But this new day, I am awake physically, I am awake spiritually. Lord, as Deborah and Barak did, I give You a song (of thanksgiving and worship).

#2. Oh my Lord Jesus, You are the King of Kings, wiser and more powerful than King Solomon. Who is like unto You, O God Almighty!

***

You know all the blessings that You gave me that might have been stolen spiritually. You know the things that have been captured out of my life while I was sleeping.

Please, Father, whatever has been stolen or exchanged from my life this last night or any night while I was sleeping - sleeping either physically or spiritually - locate them and restore them back to me now - in the name of Jesus Christ.

***

#3. Restore my health, restore my wealth.

#4. Restore any part of my body that might have been tampered with.

#5. Restore my job, my allocation, my contract, my position, my status, my promotion, my children's blessings.

#6. Restore my marriage - in the name of Jesus.

#7. Any evil exchange or mischievous trade-by-batter that might have taken place over my life, revert and restore it - in the name of Jesus Christ.

Ephesians: 4. 8-9 says:

> *Wherefore he saith, When he ascended up on high, HE LED CAPTIVITY CAPTIVE, AND GAVE GIFTS UNTO MEN.*
>
> *9. (Now that he ascended, what is it but that he also descended first into the lower parts of the earth?*

Jesus descended to the netherworld beneath and released the souls of the people and the things held in captivity.

He also ascended on high on His way to heaven and saw those whose gifts and blessings and destinies were help in captivity by forces of darkness in the air and He released the gifts unto men.

#8. Lord, send Your angels underground, inside the waters, in the forests, at any shrine or altar or in the air - everywhere my blessings are being held, release them unto me now - in the name of Jesus.

#9. Arrest the arresters of my life and return my captivity. Return what has been captured from my life.

#10. Turn again my captivity as You did for Job - in the name of Jesus Christ.

As Deborah and Barak, I have woken up. I lead my captivity captive. I arrest the thieves of my life and I capture back what has been captured - in the name of Jesus.

Prayer Session #31

DIVIDING THE KINGDOM OF THE ENEMY

Matthew: 12. 25.

> *25. And Jesus ... said unto them, Every kingdom divided against itself is brought to desolation; and every city or house divided against itself shall not stand:*
>
> *26. And if Satan cast out Satan, he is divided against himself; how shall then his kingdom stand?*

#1. Every co-operation of forces of darkness against the peace of this nation - shall fail - in the name of Jesus.

#2. Every conspiracy against this nation shall fail.

#3. Every international and internal conspiracy against the Church of God in this nation shall fail.

#4. By the power of the Holy Spirit, I decree that the enemies of peace in this nation be divided. Their kingdom will not stand. All their plans shall fail.

#5. In the name of Jesus, all those who believe they have concluded and perfected their plans to cause war in our land shall be disappointed.

#6. All those waiting to sell weapons to warring groups in our nation and third world nations shall be disappointed. Nations reported to be supplying weapons to Islamic terrorists shall be disgraced. Leaders sponsoring unrests and bloodshed in our land will not know peace.

#7. Every kingdom of Satan working against the Church of God and the innocent people to destroy them shall not stand. I command such kingdom to be divided - in the name of Jesus.

#8. O God, reveal every secret meeting and plans being made anywhere to cause massive bloodshed in this nation.

#9. God will give our land rest from all these evil people.

#10. Every hand that is joined together against my well-being, - let the hands be paralyzed - in the name of Jesus. Praise Him.

Prayer Session #32

VOMIT THEM UP

Job: 20. 15.

> *He hath swallowed down riches, and he shall vomit them up again: God shall cast them out of his belly.*

Certain spiritual entities can swallow down one's riches. Having money is not just a result of hard work or doing the right business. Neither is poverty necessarily a result of laziness or lack of opportunity or lack of business sense. In fact, money isn't just physical paper. There are spiritual dimensions to money. Money can be stolen spiritually. Wealth can be transferred or diverted spiritually. It can also be reverted or recovered back spiritually.

Scripture says "the love of money is the root of ALL EVIL." That is a serious statement. Much of the violence in our land and in the nations today has connection with money: kidnapping for ransom, kidnapping for rituals, political power rituals, robbery, and corruption in the world and in the church - are for money as the ultimate goal. In Africa, there is a spirit of *Ajé* in Yoruba land. It is the patron spirit of business people who worship the market demon. It is like the spirit of *Mammon*. Market women in South West Nigeria, for example, greet one another as "*Ajé a wá o, Ajé a wo'gbá o*", meaning, "Ajé will visit you today, she will enter your warehouse etc." The belief is that when the spirit of *Ajé* visits you, she will divert customers to you. She will make sure your wares are cleared. If you are in a market where people have employed such demons through sacrifice to help their business and you do not pray well and assert your spiritual authority in Christ, you may not sell much because those forces of darkness divert clients and customers to their shops. Your wealth can be diverted.

#1. Father, I give thanks for your faithfulness in my finances. Your Word says, "The earth is the Lord's and the fullness thereof."

#2. From this day, because I belong to you, I place a demand on the Fullness of the earth.

#3. Father, because I am your child and You own the fullness of the Earth, I shall not be limited to the wealth of this land. Because the God of the whole Earth is my Father and I am His heir, I am a global citizen.

#4. Because I am a global citizen, I refuse to be limited to the budget and resources of this land. I refuse to live as a stranger and foreigner in any part of the world.

#5. I place a demand on the wealth of nations. I place a demand on the budget of nations. I place a demand on the wealth of Asia, the wealth of the Oceania, the wealth of Africa, the wealth of Europe and Americas – in the name of Jesus.

#6. Father, open doors of businesses I need to do to access the wealth of nations.

#7. I paralyze and bind every spiritual entity that might have swallowed down my wealth.

#8. In the name of Jesus, I decree that whatever power that has swallowed down my riches, vomit it and die - in the name of Jesus.

#9. By the power of the Holy Spirit, I release my riches from satanic warehouses.

#10. I release my money from satanic strong rooms in any part of the world where they are hidden – in the name of Jesus.

#11. The sea must give up my wealth. The rivers, the forests - must release my wealth - in the name of Jesus.

#12. Every serpent that is harboring my blessing in the belly, vomit them and die - in the name of Jesus.

#13. The rod of the wicked shall no longer remain upon my lot and my allocation here and in the nations. (Psalm 125:1-5).

#14. I break that rod in the name of Jesus Christ.

#15. I release my allocation in this land. I release my allocation in the nations.

#16. My life will attract money from different parts of the world this year.

#17. I receive wisdom that is marketable in different parts of the world.

#18. My works and wisdom shall be in demand in different parts of the world.

#19. I decree that all the wicked people that have swallowed down the riches of the poor in Africa, let them begin to vomit them - in the name of Jesus.

#20. I bless the name of the Lord Jesus, the possessor of heaven and earth.

Prayer Session #33

MY GLORY AND THE LIFTER UP OF MY HEAD

Psalm: 3. 2-4.

> *Many there be which say of my soul, There is no help for him in God.*
>
> *3. But thou, O LORD, art a shield for me; my glory, and the lifter up of mine head.*
>
> *4. I cried unto the LORD with my voice, and he heard me out of his holy hill. Selah.*

#1. Father, thank you for how far you have helped me.

#2. Lord, I cry unto You, and I ask that in every area where people are saying, "there is no help for him in God", show up now - in the name of Jesus Christ.

#3. I know there is nothing You cannot do. Let my mockers begin to see Your glory in this area of my life.

#4. I refuse to lose my hope in the Almighty God.

#5. "... thou, O LORD, art a shield for me; my glory, and the lifter up of mine head."

#6. O my God, remain my shield. Remain my defense in the midst of this wicked generation. Remain a shield to my children and all family members and friends and all Your children, especially, where there is persecution of Christians.

#7. I shall not be a victim of the wickedness of this generation - in the name of Jesus Christ.

#8. My family shall not be victims of the wickedness of this land.

#9. Father, in every place I have been despised, disgraced or bowed down, lift up my head.

#10. In every place I have been dishonored or pitied, Father, show up as my glory and lifter up of my head.

#11. Lord, let all those who have looked down upon me begin to look up unto me from henceforth.

#12. Thank You, Lord, for you are my confidence, my hope, my glory and the Lifter-up of my head! Halleluyah!

Prayer Session #34

DEALING WITH
THE SPIRIT OF ABIMELECH – Part 1

Texts: Genesis 18: 9-16; Gen 20:1-20. Gen 26:6-11

9. And they (God and the two Angels that visited Abraham) said unto him, Where is Sarah thy wife? And he said, Behold, in the tent.

10. And he said, I will certainly return unto thee according to the time of life; and, lo, Sarah thy wife shall have a son. And Sarah heard it in the tent door, which was behind him.

11. Now Abraham and Sarah were old and well stricken in age; and it ceased to be with Sarah after the manner of women.

12: Therefore Sarah laughed within herself, saying, After I am waxed old shall I have pleasure, my lord being old also?*

13: And the LORD said unto Abraham, Wherefore did Sarah laugh, saying, Shall I of a surety bear a child, which am old?*

14: Is any thing too hard for the LORD? At the time appointed I will return unto thee, according to the time of life, and Sarah shall have a son.

Here, the prophecy of 25 years has just got a date of fulfillment – within the next 12 months, the baby would be born.

From that moment, God started working on the body of Sarah. The work of rejuvenating the body has started. The biochemistry of the body has started changing to facilitate pregnancy for the expected baby. All her organs and systems have started to respond to that Word from the Creator of the body.

Then, something happened!

Genesis: 20:1:

> *1. And Abraham journeyed from thence toward the south country ... and sojourned in Gerar.*
>
> *2: ..... and Abimelech king of Gerar sent, and took Sarah.*
>
> *3: But God came to Abimelech in a dream by night, and said to him, Behold, thou art but a dead man, for the woman which thou hast taken; for she is a man's wife.*
>
> *4: But Abimelech had not come near her: and he said, Lord, wilt thou slay also a righteous nation? ....*
>
> *6: And God said unto him in a dream, ...*
>
> *7: Now, therefore, restore the man his wife; for he is a prophet, and he shall pray for thee, and thou shalt live: and if thou restore her not, know thou that thou shalt surely die, thou, and all that are thine.*

8: Therefore Abimelech rose early in the morning, and called all his servants, and told all these things in their ears: and the men were sore afraid.

11: And Abraham said, Because I thought, Surely the fear of God is not in this place; and they will slay me for my wife's sake. *

Abraham apparently had not resumed sleeping with Sarah yet. Both of them had stopped that long ago. Sarah told God they were no longer "having pleasure, because my lord being old also".

But after a few weeks, when God had prepared the body of Sarah for conception, only waiting for meeting with the husband, a man called Abimelech saw Sarah and took her - to sleep with!

If he had succeeded in sleeping with Sarah, she could have conceived. The miracle son, Isaac, for which Abraham had waited for many years would have been born in the house of Abimelech and would have been given a different name with a different surname.

That is a spirit that hijacks blessings and prophecies at the point of fulfillment!

God immediately intervened and made Abimelech impotent and all those in his house.

Who is Abimelech?

He is a human being. But the name is a kingship title like Pharaoh or Herod.

i). As Pharoah or Herod, Abimelech represents a spiritual entity, a principality, territorial spirit - stronger to deal with than normal familiar spirits. It may not be the same

139

Abimelech that took Sarah that also wanted to take Rebecca, Isaac's wife. It may be his son, sitting on the same throne with the same principality working in him – as Pharaohs and Herods and all traditional rulers.

ii). Abimelech is a Husband killer. A widow producer. If you have a pretty wife, get ready to face Abimelech. If you have a good and loving husband or lover who wants to marry you, get ready to deal with Abimelech or you lose the man.

Abraham told a lie because an Abimelech was to kill him. Isaac told a lie because an Abimelech was to kill him.

PRAYER #1: My husband will not die. I will not be an untimely widow. (Even if you are single, pray this prayer in advance.)

A certain woman dealt with another Abimelech that manifested in the time of the Judges. (Judges: 9:53): *"And a certain woman cast a piece of a millstone upon Abimelech's head, ... to brake his skull."*

PRAYER #2: I release millstones and missiles upon the head of the Abimelech of my life – in the name of Jesus!

iii). Abimelech is a wife snatcher, husband snatcher;

iv). Abimelech is a Marriage destroyer. Abimelech is interested in your marriage;

v). As he attacked the marriage of Abraham, he attacked that of his son, Isaac, also. It is the spirit that attacked your father or your mother's marriage;

vi). Abimelech is a Covenant and promise hijacker.

vii). Abimelech is the power contending with prophecies in your life.

viii). Abimelech is a destiny hijacker, the spirit that gives you an alternative to the will of God.

ix). Abimelech is the spirit that wants to share you with your husband or your wife. The spirit that is interested in sharing what God has exclusively given you.

x). As your husband loves you, Abimelech is also interested in you. He may even claim to be the legitimate 'husband'. Sometimes, he would attempt to assault you sexually in dream. He may either delay marriage or contend with your husband in bed after you are married.

A couple came to me with a strange problem. The wife had a nasty experience two weeks before her wedding. Someone came to make love to her in the dream. The experience was so serious and real that she was physically disvirgined. She woke up with physical blood on bed and her body with her hymen broken!

Even though the hymen had been broken, yet for 5 months after the wedding, the husband could not penetrate - until after she underwent deliverance! After two weeks of enjoying themselves, 'Abimelech' retaliated by making the husband impotent for about a month. Then we had another deliverance session. Today, they have three children.

xi). When you are expecting a miracle, Abimelech knows about it and may give you a dream to frustrate it.

xii). Abimelech is a secret monitor of your finances. Before any good money comes in, he already creates a problem to take much of the money.

He may punish you with regular laceration on your body; he can cause regular eating in the dream – this is to serve as spiritual contraceptives, especially, during your ovulation or after you had fun with your spouse;

If you experience oppression after a hot prayer and fasting period, it may be an Abimelech monitoring you.

PRAYER: #3. FATHER, LET YOUR FIRE FALL upon my Abimelech - in the name of Jesus! (Pray this very well).

#4. In the manner of Judges 9:53, I release my bomb, my missile and millstone of fire upon Abimelech's head; I brake his skull – in the name of Jesus!

#5. Every power contending with prophecies in my life, be roasted by fire - in the name of Jesus!

#6. Every power making a claim over my marriage, I take my position in the heavenlies and exercise my authority over you - in the name of Jesus.

#7. I release my marriage from under your influence – in the name of Jesus.

#8. You spirit that is targeting to deny me of my marriage, you spirit that wants to kill my spouse, I am not your candidate. My spouse is not your candidate.

#9. You, Abimelech, husband killer, you will not touch my husband. I will not be a young widow - in the name of Jesus.

#10. You spiritual wife snatcher and wife killer, you will not operate in my family. I terminate your plans for my family. I will not be a widower - in the name of Jesus.

#11. You spirit that has been hijacking my miracle, your time is up in my life.

#12. All my long awaited miracles and promises of God that you have diverted or stolen, I command you to return them now - in the name of Jesus.

#13. As God paralyzed Abimelech and all the people in his house because of Sarah, today I paralyze and castrate all Abimelechs defiling me in my dreams - in the name of Jesus.

#14. From today, my body becomes untouchable for you. I receive fire on my body. From today, any attempt you make to touch me, you shall be electrocuted - in the name of Jesus.

#15. I pray for all Christian girls who were abducted by terrorist children of Abimelech and forcefully converted to Islam. We release you from your Abimelechs – in the name of Jesus.

#16. As fear gripped Abimelech, we release fear upon all terrorists. God says "the fear of you and the dread of you shall be upon your enemies."

#17. Give thanks to God for His omnipotence and victory over the spirit of Abimelech.

Prayer Session #35

DEALING WITH

THE SPIRIT OF ABIMELECH – Part 2

(Abimelech and Isaac)

Genesis: 26:1

1. And there was a famine in the land, beside the first famine that was in the days of Abraham. And Isaac went unto Abimelech king of the Philistines unto Gerar.

(Living in a certain location may expose you to the spirit of Abimelech)

6: And Isaac dwelt in Gerar:

7: And the men of the place asked him of his wife; and he said, She is my sister: for he feared to say, She is my wife; lest, said he, the men of the place should kill me for Rebekah; because she was fair to look upon. (ABIMELECH IS A HUSBAND KILLER).

8: And it came to pass, when he had been there a long time, that Abimelech king of the Philistines looked out at a window, and saw, and, behold, Isaac was sporting with Rebekah his wife.

*9: And Abimelech called Isaac, and said, Behold,
of a surety she is thy wife: and how saidst thou,
She is my sister?*

Whether or not Rebecca was Isaac's wife or sister, what is the business of Abimelech in this?

And Isaac said unto him, Because I said, Lest I die for her.

Who Is Abimelech?

Last time, we saw that: Abimelech symbolizes the spirit that hijacks blessing at the point of prophecy fulfillment. Abimelech is a wife snatcher, husband killer and marriage destroyer.

As he attacked the marriage of Abraham, here he attacked that of his son, Isaac, also. It is the spirit that attacked your father or your mother or some aunts in your father's house. The Abimelech that snatched Sarah some seventy to eighty years earlier might have died, but the spirit has possessed his son on the throne.

While Rebecca and Isaac were playing love, Abimelech, a king, came secretly in the middle of the night, took a ladder and was peeping through the window of this new couple!

Sometimes, you think all the doors and windows of your bedroom are locked; but there may be a spiritual window through which a spirit is watching you. You think only two of you are seeing each other; it may not be so.

Sometimes, it may not even be a peeping through a window; it may be that Abimelech is actually inside the bedroom with you and your spouse and you are not aware!

A lady who was experiencing delay in marriage once told me that after a very hot prayer session, she had a dream. In the dream, she and the husband were making love and she saw

145

that her mother-in-law was right there beside the bed with a bottle in her hand collecting the sperm of her husband as the man was ejaculating. That was 'Abimelech' inside her bedroom. That was why the woman could not conceive. What she thought was entering her womb was not really entering, but being diverted elsewhere.

PRAYER: #1. *In the name of Jesus Christ of Nazareth, every power monitoring my bedroom affairs, be roasted by fire!*

xii) Abimelech is a spirit that is peeping into your life and destiny;

> *"And it came to pass ... that Abimelech king of the Philistines looked out at a window, and saw, and, behold, Isaac was sporting with Rebekah his wife..."* (Genesis 26:8).

How can a whole king come out in the middle of the night and peeping through the window of a couple?

PRAYER #2: *Father, I close every spiritual door in my life through which Abimelech is peeing into my destiny and matrimonial life.*

xiii) Abimelech is the secret monitor of your success; he is jealous of your laughter and joy; unhappy when you are happy.

xiv). He is the secret monitor of your bedroom affairs - what you think only two of you are seeing, Abimelech is seeing it also. When you think all doors are closed and locked, Abimelech is seeing you through a spiritual window or curtain.

xv). Abimelech is a Spiritual CCTV. Sometimes, Abimelech may not be around you, but he may plant a spiritual camcorder or CCTV in your bedroom. One of my sisters told me she woke up and had a feeling she was seeing a CCTV camera at a corner of her room. Her elder sister had a dream the same night seeing the same CCTV camera in the younger sister's bedroom!

PRAYER #4: *Holy Ghost, destroy now, every spiritual CCTV camera installed in my bedroom and house – in the name of Jesus!*

Please, pray this prayer well if you think you are being monitored.

xvi). Abimelech is the spirit that monitors or eavesdrops on your prayers to know your plans. That may be one of the advantages of speaking in tongues.

When you are expecting a miracle, Abimelech may know about it and may give you a dream to frustrate it. When you are telling someone else about your expectation, Abimelech picks the information and tries to frustrate it.

If you don't mind, take a few minutes or hours tonight to deal with Abimelech. He doesn't respect prophecy or positive confession.

PRAYER #5: *I fumigate my house and my premises with the blood of Jesus - in the name of Jesus.*

Prayer Session #36

THE ANOINTING OF JEHU – Part 1

2 Kings: 9. 1-3.

> *1. And Elisha the prophet called one of the children of the prophets, and said unto him, Gird up thy loins, and take this box of oil in thine hand, and go to Ramoth-gilead:*
>
> *2. And when thou comest thither, look out there Jehu the son of Jehoshaphat the son of Nimshi, and go in, and make him arise up from among his brethren, and carry him to an inner chamber;*
>
> *3. Then take the box of oil, and pour it on his head, and say, Thus saith the LORD, I have anointed thee king over Israel. Then open the door, and flee, and tarry not.*

God had instructed Elijah to go and anoint Jehu as King of Israel. But in his haste to run away from the witchcraft of Jezebel, Elijah did not anoint Jehu (2 Kings 19:15-16).

But God did not forget Jehu. He still located him in the midst of his colleagues while they were drinking at the 'Officers Mess'. God used someone else to anoint Jehu.

#1: Father, locate me in the midst of my classmates and colleagues and anoint me.

#2: Father, in case there was someone who was supposed to be an instrument for my promotion or lifting but who has

148

forgotten me, raise another man to do it. Even if that person has left his position or is even dead, raise an alternative for me to take me to my high places in life - in the name of Jesus.

Psalm 45:7 says,

> *Thou loveth righteousness and hateth wickedness, therefore God, the God, hath anointed thee with the oil of gladness above thy fellows.*

#3: Father, anoint me with the oil of gladness above my fellows. Wipe away my tears and launch me into a new glory.

#4. Baptize me with new oil in the midst of my colleagues.

#5: Let Your anointing lift me up above those who have gone ahead of me.

#6: Jehu was anointed suddenly, unannounced. No committee was involved. Father, lift me up suddenly. Change my status suddenly.

#7: Jehu's colleagues (of the same rank) never raised any opposition to his elevation above them. They all spontaneously rose to bow before him and congratulated him.

#8. Father, silence every opposition to my promotion and elevation. Let Your new anointing and blessing upon me attract no controversy.

Promotion of a Jehu doesn't come by public opinion or by rigging. A Jehu doesn't come by nomination of political godfathers. A Jehu is selected by prophetic declaration. And once he is announced, the whole nation rises to honor him. Jehu didn't campaign for leadership. Jehu stopped the political witchcraft in Israel.

#9: O God, give us our Jehus in this nation for this moment. Give us Jehus that will not be 'anointed' and imposed upon the people by occult men, Jehus that will not be sponsored by witchcraft.

Thou loveth righteousness and hateth wickedness, therefore God, thy God, hath anointed thee above thy fellows.

#10: Father, give us Jehus that will love righteousness and justice, Jehus that will indeed hate wickedness and stop the wickedness in our land, Jehus that will not condone wickedness.

#11: Jehu was a middle aged man. Jehu "driveth furiously" (2 Kings 9:20). He is a man of action. He is self motivated, driven by passion to get things done in the shortest time. He doesn't look for excuses for delay or non performance. Jehu achieved several things within 24 hours of his anointing.

#12: Father, let the anointing for speed come upon me. I will no longer be a late achiever.

#13: Jehu achieved what Elijah did not wait to do, dealing with Jezebel, the national sponsor of witchcraft and matron of occult men in the nation.

#14: Let the reign of Jezebel over my life expire.

#15: Let the reign of Jezebel (wickedness and bloodshed) over my nation expire.

#16: Let the reign of terror of Islamic jihadists in my land and in the nations of the world expire.

Jehu was anointed by God and he did what God anointed him to do. But after some time, he began to misbehave.

#17: Father, let me finish well. Let me not take your grace for granted.

#18: I pray for all Your ministers that have been anointed for one assignment or other in the nations, let them finish well. Let there be no scandal that will destroy their good works.

#19: We worship You, Father.

Prayer Session #37

THE ANOINTING OF JEHU – Part 2

1 Kings 19:14-16

> *"....because the children of Israel have forsaken thy covenant, thrown down thine altars, and slain thy prophets with the sword; and I, [even] I only, am left; and they seek my life, to take it away.*
>
> *15 And the LORD said unto him, Go, return on thy way to the wilderness of Damascus: and when thou comest, anoint Hazael [to be] king over Syria:*
>
> *16 And Jehu the son of Nimshi shalt thou anoint [to be] king over Israel: and Elisha the son of Shaphat of Abel-meholah shalt thou anoint [to be] prophet in thy room.*

Today, we are revisiting the anointing of Jehu. I want us to repeat a major prayers in that session.

God had instructed Elijah to go towards Damascus in the wilderness where he would meet Hazael and he should anoint him as king over Syria because Ben Hadad had failed and also to go and meet Jehu to anoint him as king of Israel because Ahab had failed. But Elijah never anointed any of them till he went to heaven.

The only person he 'anointed' was Elisha. Even in the case of Elisha, Elijah didn't really anoint him. The man only 'caught' the anointing through a mantle of Elijah that fell. Elijah wasn't enthusiastic about anointing anybody. Even when Elisha was begging him and pursuing the anointing, Elijah was discouraging him and making things difficult. The conditions God didn't demand or require for this anointing were what he was giving to Elisha. His mantle only fell. He didn't deliberately anoint Elisha as God had instructed. He could have taken the anointing to heaven, even after Elisha resigned as CEO of his big farm and gave away his shares. (1 Kings 19:19-21).

Prayer #1: My Father, every power or human being that has taken my blessing to the grave, let the graves vomit them – in the name of Jesus.

#2: For all my blessings that were diverted by some people and that were never released till they died, O God, let the graves begin to surrender them to me – in the name of Jesus.

Why did Elijah not anoint the people God instructed him to anoint? Why did he refuse to release them into their destinies?

This could be a personal decision against the instruction. It could be he was overwhelmed by his own problems; it could be too much fear of the witch, Jezebel, whose security agents had spread their network in the country to arrest him.

The disobedience of Elijah delayed the promotion of Hazael and Jehu for many years. These two assignments could have been done within a month. But Jehu wasn't anointed until many years later.

Ahab was the 8th king in Israel. Jehu was 11th king! It means Jehu should have been the 9th king. He should have started ruling immediately if Elijah had anointed him king at the time God commanded.

But because Elijah hesitated, Ahab still lived for about 5 years on the throne and two of his wicked sons (Ahaziah and

Jehoram) also ruled for about 19 years altogether before Jehu was eventually anointed by Elisha.

The day Jehu was anointed was the very day he started to rule. Someone had wasted about 24 years of his destiny and reduced the period he would have spent on the throne.

Jehu was delayed at the same rank of Captain even as a fine and gallant soldier for 24 years. Eventually, he ruled for 28 years. That means if he had been anointed earlier as God instructed, he would have reigned for about 52 years. That means Jehu was destined to be one of the longest serving rulers in Israel. But someone's personal decision, inaction or reluctance delayed his destiny.

Has your life been delayed in any area of life?

#3: Father, compensate me for the years that might have been wasted in my life.

It is not every person that is denying you of your blessing or wasting your life that is a witch or a wicked person. Elijah was a prophet, not a witch. Some time-wasters don't know they are doing anything evil. Some do it deliberately. Even preachers can do it, to ground your life.

When Elijah refused to anoint Jehu, God commanded Elisha to do the job later.

#4: O God, command my promotion, my elevation, my destiny fulfillment from other sources.

#5: Father, fast track my promotion and elevation.

Prayer Session #38

SLAYING THE SACRED COWS

To slay means to kill, terminate or terminate operations.
Luke 19:12-15, 27.

> *"But those mine enemies, which would not that I should reign over them, bring hither, and slay them before me."*

The idiom 'sacred cows' is an American expression; the allusion is from Hinduism where cows are regarded as holy animals and worshipped as gods. The ancient Egyptians also worshipped cows.

The young cow (calf) that Aaron manufactured for Israelites to worship in the wilderness was to replicate the Egyptian sacred cows they left behind in Egypt. Moses smashed the golden sacred cow, burnt it and ground it into powder and cast the ashes into a brook. (Deut 9:21).

In Hindu religion in India and other places in the East, when a sacred cow misbehaves, it must not be punished. When she charges at you, kicks or even kills you, they cannot kill it. They must find a justifiable explanation for the evil action. They can say maybe a spirit of the ancestors inside the cow is trying to take revenge or punish you for an evil you did in your earlier life before you 'reincarnated'.

As an idiom, 'sacred cows' are men or women of authority; men and women above question, above criticism, above the laws of the land. They may be in religious authority, political authority, economic or business authority, traditional authority; untouchable wolves in sheep's clothing; they can be in Christianity, Islam or traditional religion; there are political sacred cows, executive and legislative thieves and honorable thugs.

Give them contracts of millions of Dollars to execute; they do half of it, abandon the rest and collect the money for everything and nobody can question them because they are party godfathers and sponsors. The same contract is rewarded to another person at higher or even double the first cost.

When a new Commissioner of Police resumes duty in a state, the sacred cows package a 'welcome gift' for him so they can do anything without any problem. You can't arrest them and you can't win a case against them, even in court.

They are the end users of the kidnapped victims for rituals. They acquire chieftaincy titles to become sacred at the traditional level.

There are many wicked people who have been decorated with garlands of national honors – CFR, OON, GCFR, etc etc., chiefs and high chiefs, blood drinkers, kings and nobles, cannibals of different titles, patrons and grand patrons of ritualists, merchants of human parts, sacred cows of robbery, sacred cows in the police and in the military, spiritual sponsors of armed robbers; Imams and prayer contractors of Yahoo-boys, sponsors of terrorists that one can never suspect, sponsors of Fulani herdsmen who are untouchable.

#1. O God, You are the only Almighty. Remove their garlands and expose them!

When Jehu was anointed, he went for the sacred cows in the land, starting from Jezebel, the head of the witches who was controlling the politics of the land. She was untouchable; but Jehu touched her.

After dealing with the politicians, Jehu went after all the priests of Baal in the nation. He summoned them from all the villages in Israel for a national 'cultural festival'. (2 Kings 10:18-28).

They represented the religious sacred cows of Israel, the untouchable clergy. Jehu slaughtered all of them and cleansed the land.

#2. Let God arise and send His angels from heaven to begin to deal with the religious sacred cows, political sacred cows, traditional sacred cows, military sacred cows in this nation.

#3. O God, Let this nation have rest from wickedness.

#4. We declare: Enough is enough!

#5. O God, expose the many altars of human sacrifices in this nation.

#6. Expose the dens of kidnappers and terrorists in this land and in nations of the world.

#7. All the sacred cows in the civil service, in the oil and gas sectors and in every sector, O God, expose and sack them.

#8. All the unrepentant sacred cows behind the mass bloodshed in Africa, O God, arise and begin to slay them if they refuse to repent.

#9.The major sacred cows who are sponsoring terrorists in Africa and in the nations of the world, Father, arise now and let the blood of the innocent begin to speak against them. Let them begin to sleep.

PERSONAL SACRED COWS

Untouchable problems. When you fast and pray on the problem, you come under more severe attacks. Untouchable disease.

A king in a parable in Luke 19:27 says: *"But those mine enemies, which would not that I should reign over them, bring hither, and slay [them] before me."*

#10. Every power that says Jesus will not rule in my life, in my health, in my finances, in my marriage, in my children, in my spouse, I bring you before the throne of God and decimate your power at His feet.

Prayer Session #39

I WILL GET TO MY ROME - 1

Acts: 23. 11-24

11. And the night following the Lord stood by him, and said, Be of good cheer, Paul: for as thou hast testified of me in Jerusalem, so must thou bear witness also at Rome.

12. And when it was day, certain of the Jews banded together, and bound themselves under a curse, saying that they would neither eat nor drink till they had killed Paul.

13. And they were more than forty which had made this conspiracy.

14. And they came to the chief priests and elders, and said, We have bound ourselves under a great curse, that we will eat nothing until we have slain Paul.

15. Now therefore ye with the council signify to the chief captain that he bring him down unto you tomorrow, as though ye would inquire something more perfectly concerning him: and we, or ever he come near, are ready to kill him.

16. And when Paul's sister's son heard of their lying in wait, he went and entered into the castle, and told Paul.

17. Then Paul called one of the centurions unto him, and said, Bring this young man unto the chief captain: for he hath a certain thing to tell him.

18. So he took him, and brought him to the chief captain, and said, Paul the prisoner called me unto him, and prayed me to bring this young man unto thee, who hath something to say unto thee.....

22. So the chief captain then let the young man depart, and charged him, See thou tell no man that thou hast shewed these things to me.

23. And he called unto him two centurions, saying, Make ready two hundred soldiers to go to Caesarea, and horsemen threescore and ten, and spearmen two hundred, at the third hour of the night;

24. And provide them beasts, that they may set Paul on, and bring him safe unto Felix the governor.

God had just spoken to Paul to promise that He would make sure he gets to Europe to do ministry. But immediately after the revelation of God, certain wicked men plotted to kill him to prevent this and ground his ministry.

#1. In the name of Jesus Christ, I will get to my Rome.

#2. Whatever is the plot of the wicked against the plan of God for my life, they shall fail - in the name of Jesus.

#3. Wherever I have to be to fulfill my destiny, I shall be there in the name of Jesus.

Paul had a good dream and revelation about God's plan for his life. But certain people were inspired by demons to destroy the dream.

#4. I decree in the name of Jesus, every power that always hijacks dreams and God's purpose for my life, be disgraced.

Over 40 assassins bound themselves by "a great curse" to kill Paul. To bind oneself under a curse is to invite some supernatural forces to strike or destroy one if one violates or fails to carry out the plan. These people vowed not to eat or drink anything till after killing Paul. Paul escaped by night. So these people would either die of hunger and dehydration or if they break the vow by eating later, the great curse would catch up with them.

#5. Father, all those who have vowed themselves for my destruction will be caught in their vows.

#6. Let every oath taken against my life and family catch up with the oath makers.

#7. Let the demons they have employed in their oaths and curses turn against them.

Over 40 men laid ambush against Paul. They waited in vain. Paul had escaped by 9pm before the enemies woke up in the morning!

#8. I will escape all the ambushes of the enemy against my life and family - in the name of Jesus.

#9. Every power laying ambush against my life, you will wait in vain - in the name of Jesus.

#10. Every power waiting for my shame and disgrace this month will wait in vain.

Paul's nephew was either around when the evil plot was being planned or he somehow picked the information. The plot was leaked, somehow, and botched.

#11. O Father of light and Revealer of secrets, I pray that You reveal to me by revelation or by human agency any plan or conspiracy against my life - in the name of Jesus.

The enemies of Paul had perfected their plans and sealed them with a great curse upon themselves if they failed.

#12. Father, no matter how much the enemies have perfected their plans against me and my family, let them fail.

#13. This year, I shall get to my Rome (Rome can be your marriage, promotion, a country or any location you have to be to fulfill your destiny).

> *22. So the chief captain then let the young man depart, and charged him, See thou tell no man that thou hast shewed these things to me.*

> *23. And he called unto him two centurions, saying, Make ready two hundred soldiers to go to Caesarea, and horsemen threescore and ten, and spearmen two hundred, at the third hour of the night;*

> *24. And provide them beasts, that they may set Paul on, and bring him safe unto Felix the governor.*

The Brigade Commander or (General Officer Commanding the Brigade) of the city heard about this evil plot and commanded two army Colonels to mobilize 200 combatant foot soldiers plus 70 military vehicles with fighters inside, plus another 200 soldiers who were specially trained in spears. These add up to 470 soldiers to form an escort to secure a single man of God!

#14. Father, release more of Your Angels as my escorts everywhere I go. Let them go ahead of me, go with me and go behind me. Let them always clear the way for me.

#15. Let me never fall into the hands of highway robbers and terrorists.

#16. My going out and my coming in shall be safe and secure throughout this year.

#17. This year, I shall not be mourned and I shall not mourn anyone.

#18. Any evil that is programmed for me this year shall not come to pass - in the name of Jesus.

#19. All Islamic forces who have vowed themselves to be troubling Nigeria and Nigerian Christians, God shall trouble them.

#20. Those laying ambush waiting to strike the innocent, let the forests of our nation consume them.

The Brigade Commander also provided "beasts (vehicles) that they may set Paul on and bring him safe to Felix the governor..."

#21. This year, I shall be dignified-in the name of Jesus Christ.

The Army Chief didn't know Paul. Yet he did everything in his power to help him. In fact, the security he provided for Paul was more than any Governor in America or Nigeria would have, not even the Prime Minister of UK would have such honor and security!

#22. This year, great men I do not know will give me extraordinary help me - in the name of Jesus Christ.

Halleluyah! Give him praise.

I WILL GET TO MY ROME - 2

Acts: 23. 11-24

> *11. And the night following the Lord stood by him, and said, Be of good cheer, Paul: for as thou hast testified of me in Jerusalem, so must thou bear witness also at Rome.*
>
> *12. And when it was day, certain of the Jews banded together, and bound themselves under a curse, saying that they would neither eat nor drink till they had killed Paul.*
>
> *13. And they were more than forty which had made this conspiracy.*
>
> *14. And they came to the chief priests and elders, and said, We have bound ourselves under a great curse, that we will eat nothing until we have slain Paul.*

It is very important to note that it was the morning after Jesus appeared in the night to announce His plan for Paul's ministry that these evil men arose to enter into a covenant to eliminate Paul. This is not a coincidence. It simply shows that when an opposition rises suddenly against you, it is really against God's plan for your life. It means the enemy may have got inkling about the purpose of God for your life.

These wicked men were not there when Jesus was speaking to Paul. It was in a dream or revelation. But their father, the devil

(John 8:44), picked the information somehow. He was the one that inspired them to eliminate the Apostle fast.

Certain people can be directly inspired by evil spirits against you; their action may not be because of any personal offence.

#1. I Worship You, my Lord for Your plans for my life.

#2. Your perfect will shall be done in my life.

#3. No power shall be able to frustrate Your purpose in my life.

#4. Every human being that has been possessed by evil spirits to thwart the plans of God in my life, I release such a person from such influences - in the name of Jesus.

#5. Every power eavesdropping into God's plan for my life, I destroy and disconnect your spiritual antennal in my vicinity - in the name of Jesus.

The first thing Jesus told Paul in that revelation was, "Be of good cheer..." It means "Don't be downcast again, don't be discouraged again, be cheerful, be excited, begin to celebrate, start dancing. You are going to Europe to preach there..."

Then as he woke up a few hours later, he got the news of assassination plot - over 40 people under a great oath to kill him!

Naturally, his joy would fade away and his countenance would change immediately.

#6. Every power contending with the joy of the Lord in my life, be disgraced - in the name of Jesus Christ.

#7. Every power contending with my good dreams, be disgraced.

#8. Every banding together against the plan and purpose of God for my life and those of my family members, let the hosts of heaven disband them by fire.

#9. O God, put them in disarray.

Note that those who "banded together" with "a great curse" to kill Paul were not atheists or herbalists, really. They were "certain Jews" and they received moral mandate from "chief priests and elders."

Sometimes, your enemies are not herbalists or idol worshippers who don't come to church. There are "certain Jews" inside church. They also believe in Jehovah. There are indeed bands of wicked men and women even inside church.

#10. Father, all those in my church with evil hearts, dressing well on Sunday but banding together for evil in the secret, visit them with a change of heart.

#11. Those who refuse to repent, visit them with your judgment. (Rev. 2:21-23).

#12. In the name of Jesus Christ, any banding together in the Islamic world against the Church of Jesus Christ will not prosper.

The devil raised 40 enemies against Paul. But God raised 470 soldiers to defend and protect him! That means at least 11 soldiers to engage one enemy and 30 others to be on guard and reserves and be commanding the fight! Glory to God!

#13. O God, for every terrorist the devil has raised up in our nation and nations of the world, raise at least 11 hosts of heaven to engage them.

#14. Begin to declare God's purpose concerning your life. Every good dream He has given you in the past, begin to declare them into reality. Begin to see yourself on your way to your own Rome.

#15. Worship Him as the Almighty God, the One who promises and will never fail.

Prayer Session #41

BETHESDA

(HOUSE OF MERCY) - Part 1

John: 5. 2-10.

> *Now there is at Jerusalem by the sheep market a pool, which is called in the Hebrew tongue Bethesda, having five porches.*
>
> *3. In these lay a great multitude of impotent folk, of blind, halt, withered, waiting for the moving of the water.*
>
> *4. For an angel went down at a certain season into the pool, and troubled the water: whosoever then first after the troubling of the water stepped in was made whole of whatsoever disease he had.*
>
> *5. And a certain man was there, which had an infirmity thirty and eight years.*
>
> *6. When Jesus saw him lie, and knew that he had been now a long time in that case, he saith unto him, Wilt thou be made whole?*
>
> *7. The impotent man answered him, Sir, I have no man, when the water is troubled, to put me into the pool: but while I am coming, another steppeth down before me.*

8. Jesus saith unto him, Rise, take up thy bed, and walk.

9. And immediately the man was made whole, and took up his bed, and walked: and on the same day was the Sabbath.

10. The Jews therefore said unto him that was cured, It is the Sabbath day: it is not lawful for thee to carry thy bed.

#Song: I will sing of the mercies of the Lord forever I will sing of the mercies of the Lord. With my mouth will I make known Thy faithfulness, thy faithfulness. With my mouth will I make known Thy faithfulness to all generations. I will sing of the mercies of the Lord forever I will sing of the mercies of the Lord.

#1. I praise the Almighty God for His mercies I have enjoyed over the years.

The name of this place is called Bethesda, which means 'House of Mercy'. But the sick man could not find mercy from all the people around him.

"... great multitude of impotent folk, of blind, halt, withered, waiting for the moving of the water..."

For multitudes of people in life, the last 5 - 15 years of their life are spent in blindness; some with stroke, dementia, amnesia and other brain or memory problems.

#2. In the name of Jesus, I will not be impotent in any area of life. I will not be blind. I will not have any eye problem. I will not be crippled. My hand will not whither. My feet will not whither. My brain will not whither. I will not have any form of stroke.

#3. I will not spend the last days of my life in pains and afflictions.

A song writer says:

>#1. Pass me not, O gentle Savior,
> Hear my humble cry;
>While on others Thou art calling,
> Do not pass me by.
>
>*Savior, Savior, Hear my humble cry;*
>*While on others Thou art calling,*
>*Do not pass me by.*
>
>2. Let me at Thy throne of mercy,
>Find a sweet relief;
>Kneeling there in deep contrition,
>Help my unbelief.
>
>3. Trusting only in Thy merit,
>Would I seek Thy face;
>Heal my wounded, broken spirit,
>Save me by Thy grace.
>
>4. Thou the spring of all my comfort,
>More than life to me;
>Whom have I on earth beside Thee?
>Whom in heaven but Thee?

#4. O God, do not let Your mercy pass me by.

>*5. And a certain man was there, which had an infirmity thirty and eight years.*
>
>*6. When Jesus saw him lie, and knew that he had been now a long time in that case, he saith unto him, Wilt thou be made whole?"*

This man was not the only man that was sick. All the multitudes there were very sick. But it was his own problem that attracted the attention and mercy of Jesus.

#5. Father, let my problem attract Your attention.

The man told Jesus that the reason why he had remained in that condition for 38 years was because *"I have no man ... to put me into the pool."*

#6. Father, give me a man. Give me men. Give me a woman - to lift me from my present state and condition to another state.

The man was a few meters away from his miracle source - the healing pool, but helpless to get there. There are many people who are close to their miracle but cannot get it. If this man had not been helped by Jesus, he would have died beside that miracle water.

#7. Father, I will not die beside my miracle.

If this man had died beside the pool, the multitudes who did not carry him into the pool would have carried his dead body away from that place to a longer distance - burial ground - which may be miles away - to bury him - to prevent decay and smell near them. But while he was alive and needed their help to carry him for just a few meters, they were unwilling to do that.

Sometimes, some "helpers" come only after one's death. Senator Joseph of Arimathea donated a sepulcher to Jesus after His death. He never built a house for Jesus when He was alive. Jesus was "like a fox, (that) had no place to lay His head." A ruler of the synagogue, Nicodemus, bought a new white cloth to wrap the dead body of Jesus. He never bought a garment for Jesus when He was alive. When a man dies, people who never gave him money in life would be ready to donate money for casket, grave clothes and other funeral expenses.

#8. Father, let my helpers come now while I am still alive.

"I have no man to carry me." But Jesus saith unto him, "Rise, take up thy bed and walk..."

#9. By the Lord Jesus, I am rising this day, from my present bed of limitation, bed of stagnancy, bed of affliction, bed of loneliness, in the name of Jesus.

Verse 10: *"The Jews therefore said unto him that was cured, 'It is the Sabbath day; it is not lawful for thee to carry thy bed...'*

Was it lawful to be bedridden and be in pain on the Sabbath?

What good thing has the enemy made "unlawful" for you? Good job? Marriage? You must break those "Sabbaths" today.

#10. Every good thing that forces of darkness have made unlawful for me, I break their laws today – in the name of Jesus.

This man did not know Jesus (verse 13).

#11. Men and women I do not know will help me.

Prayer Session #42

BETHESDA (HOUSE OF MERCY) - 2

John: 5. 1-3

> *After this there was a feast of the Jews; and Jesus went up to Jerusalem.*
>
> *2. Now there is at Jerusalem by the sheep market a pool, which is called in the Hebrew tongue Bethesda, having five porches.*
>
> *3. In these lay a great multitude of impotent folk, of blind, halt, withered, waiting for the moving of the water.*

While 'a great multitude' of people were suffering in pains and agony, a religious feast was going on very close by.

Nobody cared about the suffering masses. All those passing by to the temple for feast saw the man who had been in pain for 38 years and they pretended they didn't see him. Even if they had no anointing to heal him, they could help to carry him into the miracle pool. But nobody cared. Religious ceremonies were more important to them than helping the needy. Even when Jesus saw the man and helped him, the religious people were offended that Jesus and the sick person broke the law of Sabbath!

We still have such hypocrisy today. There are multitudes in the church and near us as neighbors who are greatly in need. But we are more occupied with religious activities and feasts and conventions and anniversaries costing us millions.

#1. Lord, have mercy on me if I had ignored those I could help.

#2. Have mercy on my church if we have been ignoring those suffering in the church and around us.

#3. Have mercy on us as a wealthy and highly endowed nation of religious people where trillions are changing hands every day and yet 'great multitudes' are suffering.

#4. Father, as I am praying to you to send me helpers, make me also a helper.

#5. Open my eyes this month to see the people in church and in my neighborhood that I can be a blessing to.

#6. Make me an answer to someone's prayers this month.

#7. Lord, let our churches become true Bethesdas (houses of mercy) for the needy and no more houses of exploitation of the needy.

Verse 4-6.

> *"... whosoever then first after the troubling of the water stepped in was made whole of whatsoever disease he had."*

Then the anointing would expire. Nobody knew when next the angel would come back.

> *7. The impotent man answered him, Sir, I have no man, when the water is troubled, to put me into the pool: but while I am coming, another steppeth down before me.*

Bethesda was a place of competition. Even though it was a 'house of mercy', the mercy available was not sufficient for everybody.

But the man who had no man to help and who had been disadvantaged for years was the only person Jesus helped and He left other selfish people there to continue their competition.

#8. Lord Jesus, give me an advantage over my competitors.

#9. Single my case out in the midst of the multitudes.

> *"...while I am coming, another steppeth down before me..."*

The man had tried many times and saw that his efforts were useless. Somebody was always beating him to it. He then didn't try again. He lay on the mat there waiting to die one day. He could not stand up and walk home. He would have died beside the healing pool in a state of hopelessness and despair.

#9. Father, whatever opportunity I have lost to my competitors, I regain them now, in the name of Jesus.

Those who expected the man to die beside the pool were shocked when they saw him in the temple. He had not been in the service for 38 years and nobody cared. They would all have come to conduct his funeral service. But they were disappointed seeing him standing and dancing in the temple.

#10. Those who have concluded I would die this way will be disappointed very soon.

#11. I will appear soon to the surprise of many.

We are in a nation where the poor and the innocent are dying and the wicked are being guarded by armed police officers.

#12. The Lord will arise to help the afflicted. The Lord will arise and help the church in this country.

#13. Those who have refused to help us shall be disappointed - in the name of Jesus.

Prayer Session #43

COMPENSATION - 1

*When **the Lord saw** that Leah was unloved, He opened her womb; but Rachel was barren (Gen. 29:31).*

Because Jacob came from Abraham, it was possible he might have inherited whatever caused the delay of child bearing that Abraham his grandfather and Isaac and Rebecca his father and mother had.

Jacob's 'real' preferred wife, Rachel, became barren. Womb closed. Leah, the first wife, too might have married the curse of delay. Her womb too might have been closed by that curse of delay. But "when the LORD saw that Leah was hated, He opened her womb; but Rachel was barren."

If the womb were not closed, there would have been no need to open it. So, it seems Leah married into a family of closed wombs. But God compensated her for this hatred she suffered from a man she had given her body, and probably her virginity.

Have you been hated by someone you have shown love? Have you been rewarded evil for good you have shown? Have you been despised by someone you admired?

Say, "O my Father in Heaven, compensate me."

May be Leah prayed, "Lord, look at me, what did I do? I did not force myself on this man. This marriage was not arranged by me. When I found myself in this marriage, I accepted Jacob as husband. When he was sleeping with me, he pretended he didn't know my identity. After all, he was hearing my voice.

We did not sleep in darkness. I was not in a *hijab* when he was sleeping with me."

Leah loved Jacob and was devoted to him throughout their marriage. She was rewarded by God through Judah from whom Jesus came and Levi through whom the priesthood was established.

Have you suffered rejection from your husband, wife, boss and other people around you? Ask the Lord to compensate you.

Say: Father, in the name of Jesus, compensate me for whatever delay and deprivations I have suffered in life.

When Jacob's mummy, Rebecca, had a delay of 19 years, God compensated her with a set of twins.

When Elizabeth suffered delay for many years, God compensated her with a son that became a national prophet, whom Jesus qualified as one greater than any prophet born of men.

When Hannah suffered delay for many years, God honored her with a national prophet, priest and kingmaker in Israel.

When Job suffered heavy financial losses and breakdown in health, the Lord compensated him to have double what he lost.

Think about all the financial losses or delay in your finances over the years and ask for compensation.

#1. Father, for all the relationships I have lost, let there be compensations.

#2. For all the opportunities of jobs and contracts I lost, Father, compensate me and my family.

#3. For all the years we have suffered from bad political leadership in this country, let God have mercy on us and compensate us with altruistic and visionary leaders.

Prayer Session #44

COMPENSATION – 2

Gen. 29:31:

> *"When GOD SAW that Leah was hated, He opened her womb"*

Lesson: God sees what is going on in my family. He sees the pretending partner. He sees the wicked spouse. He sees the traitor, the deceiving partner. He sees the faithful. He sees the partner putting in his or her best to make the marriage work. God is interested in my love life. Scripture says, "He that finds a wife has found a good thing and obtains favor of the Lord." (Prov 18:22). Any man who proposed to a lady with all the sweet words in this world and won her heart and her love and later begins to show hatred towards her makes himself a traitor. Any woman who prayed to God to have a husband and after marriage begins to mistreat the man is a traitor. God sees what is going on in every marriage. He has the right to look at what is going on in every marriage because He was the one who created the institution. He has the right to inspect it

> *"When **the Lord SAW** that Leah was hated..."*

#1. Lord, see all the injustices I have suffered, the deprivations I have suffered, the rejections I have suffered, the insults I have borne, the disgrace I have suffered – and do something about my case this year.

When Leah received her first child as a compensation for the rejection she was suffering from her husband, she named the boy, "Reuben, because she said the Lord has looked upon **my affliction** ..." (Gen 30:32).

When a married and faithful woman is not loved by the husband, it is an affliction.

#2: Father, deliver me from any form of affliction I am experiencing in my matrimonial life.

She said, the Lord "looked upon" her affliction and then gave her a miracle.

#3. Father, look upon my affliction and any disgrace I am suffering. Deliver me from any mental or emotional affliction I am going through in marriage or in office or in the neighborhood - in the name of Jesus.

#4. Father, deliver me from any affliction in my health.

> *V.33: "And she conceived again and bare a son: and she said because the Lord has HEARD that I WAS HATED, He has therefore given me this son also, and she called his name Simeon"*

#5. For my shame, I shall receive double-in the name of Jesus.

God did not only "see"; He "looked upon", and He "heard" all that Leah was going through and He came to compensate her.

#6. Father, let my problems attract Your attention this year, and let there be a divine intervention - in the name of Jesus.

> *V.34: "And she conceived again, and bare a son and said, "Now this time will my husband be JOINED unto me..."*

This is strange. They had lived together for years in the same house, but not really joined in the mind, not even in the body. Rachel was the one in charge of all bedroom affairs. Leah had to borrow Jacob or pay for a night before she could have Jacob for a night. She was not really joined with her husband. Many families are in this condition - joined in the church wedding service or in the marriage registry, but not really joined in purpose, in love and in vision.

When Leah gave birth to the 6th son, she said, *"Now God has ENDUED me with a DOWRY; now will my husband DWELL with me..."* (Gen 30:12).

This was about 15 years after marriage. They were living in the same house but not "dwelling together". Rachel was the one controlling the bedroom and Leah was like a stranger or concubine in the house. That is what I call LAT – Living Apart Together or 'lating'. Many couples are living not only in separate rooms, but in separate worlds in the same house.

It was after the sixth child that she just got 'a dowry'! It was this time that Leah was just having a sense of being really married – after 15 years!

#7. Father, correct every anomaly in my marriage.

#8: Every area I am pretending is alright that is causing trouble in my marriage, help me today to put it right so my marriage will be a good testimony.

#9. Lord, I pray for all families in my church who are living in the same houses but not truly 'dwelling' together. Whatever are the walls of partition between the spouses, let the walls crumble today - in the name of Jesus.

#10. Father, let every spirit causing pain and troubles and tears in my marriage be exposed and disgraced - in the name of Jesus.

#11. Father, I thank You for a new beginning in my marriage from today.

Prayer Session #45

ANOINTING TO FORBID

1 Kings: 21. 1-21:

1. And it came to pass after these things, that Naboth the Jezreelite had a vineyard, which was in Jezreel, hard by the palace of Ahab king of Samaria.

2. And Ahab spake unto Naboth, saying, Give me thy vineyard, that I may have it for a garden of herbs, because it is near unto my house: and I will give thee for it a better vineyard than it; or, if it seems good to thee, I will give thee the worth of it in money.

3. And Naboth said to Ahab, The LORD forbid it me, that I should give the inheritance of my fathers unto thee.

4. And Ahab came into his house heavy and displeased because of the word which Naboth the Jezreelite had spoken to him: for he had said, I will not give thee the inheritance of my fathers. And he laid him down upon his bed, and turned away his face, and would eat no bread.

5. But Jezebel his wife came to him, and said unto him, Why is thy spirit so sad, that thou eatest no bread?

6. And he said unto her, Because I spake unto Naboth the Jezreelite, and said unto him, Give me thy vineyard for money; or else, if it please thee, I will give thee another vineyard for it: and he answered, I will not give thee my vineyard.

7. And Jezebel his wife said unto him, Dost thou now govern the kingdom of Israel? arise, and eat bread, and let thine heart be merry: I will give thee the vineyard of Naboth the Jezreelite.

8. So she wrote letters in Ahab's name, and sealed them with his seal, and sent the letters unto the elders and to the nobles that were in his city, dwelling with Naboth.

9. And she wrote in the letters, saying, Proclaim a fast, and set Naboth on high among the people:

10. And set two men, sons of Belial, before him, to bear witness against him, saying, Thou didst blaspheme God and the king. And then carry him out, and stone him, that he may die.

11. And the men of his city, even the elders and the nobles who were the inhabitants in his city, did as Jezebel had sent unto them, and as it was written in the letters which she had sent unto them.

12. They proclaimed a fast, and set Naboth on high among the people.

13. And there came in two men, children of Belial, and sat before him: and the men of Belial witnessed against him, even against Naboth, in the presence of the people, saying, Naboth did blaspheme God and the king. Then they carried him forth out of the city, and stoned him with stones, that he died.

14. Then they sent to Jezebel, saying, Naboth is stoned, and is dead.

15. And it came to pass, when Jezebel heard that Naboth was stoned, and was dead, that Jezebel said to Ahab, Arise, take possession of the vineyard of Naboth the Jezreelite, which he refused to give thee for money: for Naboth is not alive, but dead.

16. And it came to pass, when Ahab heard that Naboth was dead, that Ahab rose up to go down to the vineyard of Naboth the Jezreelite, to take possession of it.

17. And the word of the LORD came to Elijah the Tishbite, saying,

18. Arise, go down to meet Ahab king of Israel, which is in Samaria: behold, he is in the vineyard of Naboth, whither he is gone down to possess it.

19. And thou shalt speak unto him, saying, Thus saith the LORD, Hast thou killed, and also taken possession? And thou shalt speak unto him, saying, Thus saith the LORD, In the place where dogs licked the blood of Naboth shall dogs lick thy blood, even thine.

20. And Ahab said to Elijah, Hast thou found me, O mine enemy? And he answered, I have found thee: because thou hast sold thyself to work evil in the sight of the LORD.

21. Behold, I will bring evil upon thee, and will take away thy posterity, and will cut off from Ahab him that pisseth against the wall, and him that is shut up and left in Israel."

It is one thing to just know our rights and claim them only by mouth. It is another thing to actually claim them in reality. Naboth knew his right, but did not have the power to claim it. He had mouth but didn't have fire upon his tongue to reject evil. He didn't have the power to retain his inheritance. He knew the Scripture that says one's inheritance must not be taken by another (Lev. 25:23-24).

He could easily and boldly say to a king, "God forbid that I should give you my inheritance..." But God did not forbid it. Why?

Jesus said, *"I give unto you the keys of the kingdom of heaven; whatsoever you forbid on earth is forbidden in heaven and whatever you permit on earth, shall be permitted in heaven..."* (NLT)

It takes "the keys of the kingdom" to forbid things on earth before heaven can execute the forbidding. Naboth didn't have the keys.

If Elijah were there and he had said, "God forbid", heaven would have responded. Why? He had the power to forbid. A few years earlier when Elijah came out of the wilderness to forbid rain from falling "according to my word", heaven was closed over a whole nation for over 3 years. He had the anointing to forbid.

#1. Father, I apply for the anointing to forbid. (Pray this very well).

You had a bad dream. You woke up and say, "God forbid. I reject it in Jesus name. It shall not come to pass. That is not my portion. I cancel it in Jesus name..."

184

But the evil you saw in the dream became a reality.

It means even though you had said, 'God forbid', it was not forbidden in heaven.

It takes certain keys before heaven responds to verbal forbidding.

If we are not strong in the Lord and in the power of His might, positive confessions won't forbid certain evils. It is possible for forces of darkness or even some human beings with authority can take our "vineyards" - whether inherited or acquired.

Pray again:

#2. Lord Jesus, release upon me a new anointing to forbid; a new anointing to release. (Don't pray this casually. Sooner or later, your life may depend on it).

King Ahab said, "Give me YOUR vineyard..."

He didn't deny that Naboth was the owner. But he wanted it.

What is your vineyard that the enemy is interested in?

It may be your means of regular income, your good relationships, your marriage, your job, your position, your promotion, your national wealth, your rights in your place of work, your wealth or your health, your money or your life.

#3: Father, whatever demand is being made in the kingdom of darkness over my life, I reject the demands - in the name of Jesus.

#4. Every principality making a demand on my inheritance, be paralyzed and overthrown - in the name of Jesus.

#5. Every principality making a demand on the vineyards of the Naboths of this nation, the forces saying, "Give us your vineyards or lose your lives", O God, arise on behalf of our Naboths and defend them – in the name of Jesus!

A Nigerian presidential media spokesman told Nigerians on a TV program, "Give your ancestral land (to Fulani herdsmen for ranches) or lose your lives)." (Kakaki, AIT July 4, 2018).

#6. In the name of Jesus Christ we forbid this evil. Let heaven scatter them, in the name of Jesus!

#7. O God, arise and fight for us over our inheritance.

Are there are some things you need to forbid in your life and family and nation today? Go ahead and do so now

#8. I reject the spirit of fear and intimidation.

#9. I refuse to submit to any unjust and wicked legislation over my life and over my nation - in the name of Jesus.

#10. I will not be a victim of the wickedness of this land.

#11. Spirits of denial and deprivation in my life, your time has expired. Get out of my ways - in the name of Jesus Christ.

#12. This month, I will not be a victim of error, omission or oversight.

#13. Worship the King of kings.

Prayer Session #46

DELIVERANCE FROM WORD TORMENTORS

Judges: 16. 16-17.

16 And it came to pass, when she pressed him daily with her words, and urged him, so that his soul was vexed unto death;

17. That he told her all his heart, and said unto her. There hath not come a razor upon mine head; for I have been a Nazarite unto God from my mother's womb: if I be shaven, then my strength will go from me, and I shall become weak, and be like any other man.

Words are weapons of warfare. Most wars begin from words. Some wars are initiated, fought and won or lost only at the word level. All or at least most spiritual warfare are fought by words.

Before this time, Samson was never defeated by any physical army. Even as a single man against whole armies, he was a conqueror.

But the enemy tried another weapon - an alluring woman armed with certain words.

It wasn't just 'love' or emotions that overpowered Samson as we always say.

The lady *"pressed him daily with her words and urged him so that his soul was vexed to death."*

At this level, he felt like his life was ebbing away if he still held to his secret. This is word witchcraft.

Some of us have been compelled to say certain things that have put us into serious trouble.

#1. Father, deliver me from any bondage I have brought on myself through my own words.

#2. Father, deliver me from any negative words my life, my health, my marriage, my children, my finances and my destiny have been responding to.

Samson's "soul was vexed unto death" through words. Some people have gone to commit suicide through certain words they have heard.

#3. Father, in the name of Jesus, I release my soul from any vexation of words.

#4. I refuse to be controlled or tormented by negative words of men - in the name of Jesus.

Through those words of oppression, Samson told this evil woman "all his heart."

It is not every time we have to say all our heart in order to satisfy someone or to prove a point. Scripture says, "A fool utters all his mind: but a wise man keeps it in till afterwards" (Prov. 29:11).

#5. Father, forgive me for any folly I have displayed by giving any strategic information to my enemy.

#6. I withdraw any information about my life that is being used to control my life - in the name of Jesus.

#8. The word of the Lord is a lamp unto my feet and the navigator of my destiny.

SPORT MINISTRY

(When Ministry or Prayer Becomes Sport)

Judges: 16. 19-30:

> *19. And she (Delilah) made him (Samson) sleep upon her knees; and she called for a man, and she caused him to shave off the seven locks of his head; and she began to afflict him,* **and his strength went from him.**
>
> *20. And she said, The Philistines be upon thee, Samson. And he awoke out of his sleep, and said,* **I will go out as at other times before, and shake myself. And he knew not that the LORD was departed from him.**
>
> *21. But the Philistines took him, and put out his eyes, and brought him down to Gaza, and bound him with fetters of brass; and he did grind in the prison house.*
>
> *22. Howbeit the hair of his head began to grow again after he was shaven.*
>
> *23. Then the lords of the Philistines gathered them together for to offer a great sacrifice unto Dagon their god, and to rejoice: for they said, Our god hath delivered Samson our enemy into our hand.*

24. And when the people saw him, they praised their god: for they said, Our god hath delivered into our hands our enemy, and the destroyer of our country, which slew many of us.

25. And it came to pass, when their hearts were merry, that they said, **Call for Samson, that he may make us sport.** *And they called for Samson out of the prison house;* **and he made them sport***: and they set him between the pillars.*

26. And Samson said unto the lad that held him by the hand, Suffer me that I may feel the pillars whereupon the house standeth, that I may lean upon them.

27. Now the house was full of men and women; and all the lords of the Philistines were there; and there were upon the roof about **three thousand men and women, that beheld while Samson made sport***.*

28. **And Samson called unto the LORD, and said, O Lord GOD, remember me, I pray thee, and strengthen me***, I pray thee, only this once, O God, that I may be at once avenged of the Philistines for my two eyes.*

29. And Samson took hold of the two middle pillars upon which the house stood, and on which it was borne up, of the one with his right hand, and of the other with his left.

30. And Samson said, Let me die with the Philistines. And he bowed himself with all his might; and the house fell upon the lords, and upon all the people that were therein. So the

dead which he slew at his death were more than
they which he slew in his life.

When Samson lost the anointing, every other thing he did as 'ministration' was regarded as sport, an entertainment.

He said, "I will go out as before and SHAKE MYSELF, but he knew not that the Lord had departed from him."

Anointing simply means when God is with a man or woman to do anything. When God departs, every shaking becomes sport; all somersaults, acrobatics and pulpit theatricals become sports.

Without God's presence, my singing, instrumentation and dancing and sweating become sports.

#1. Lord, I plead with You, do not depart from me for a moment.

#2. Give me grace to run away from anything that can cause You to depart from me.

It is possible to run and grow a church or ministry without God, without anointing - once you put a system in place.

#3. Ha! O God, forbid that I should do a work in Your name without Your presence!

Samson was brought into an Amphitheatre - a kind of indoor stadium filled with 3,000 idolaters, occult men and witches - a great and rare free opportunity for evangelistic ministry. But because God was not with him, all his actions, his shakings, his words, were sports, amusements, entertainment, jokes. And everybody was laughing and dancing to his entertainment.

#4. Holy Spirit, I don't want to take Your presence for granted.

When we shout and scream against evil spirits and they don't depart, it is because they regard our prayers as sport.

When witches operate and thrive successfully in our congregation despite our prayers, it is because they regard our praying as sport.

#5. In the name of Jesus Christ, my praying and 'tonguing' will not turn to sports.

#6. Fathcr, I apply again for Your fire upon my tongue - in the name of Jesus.

> 28. And Samson called unto the LORD, and said, O Lord GOD, remember me, I pray thee, and strengthen me....,

#7. O My Father God, strengthen me again!

Having learnt his lessons and repented, Samson prayed for vengeance and God answered. What if he had prayed first that his eyes be restored and the angels of God should deliver him? It wouldn't have cost God any extra effort. God could have delivered him while the building collapsed on the enemies. God might have even converted the enemies if he had preached to them. But Samson only had anointing; he had no message.

#8. In the name of Jesus, I will not die on the battlefield. I will not die with my enemies. I will not be a laughing stock to the enemies of God.

#9. The enemy will not write the last chapter of my life - in the name of Jesus.

#10. David says, "Though I walk through the valley of the shadow of death, I shall fear no evil; for Thou art with me. Thy rod and thy staff they shall comfort me." Whatever I am going through is a walking through; I am coming out – in the name of Jesus. I will not die in this valley.

Prayer Session #48

TRIBULATION TO THE TROUBLERS

> *"Seeing it is a righteous thing with God to recompense tribulation to them that trouble you: and to you who are troubled REST with us, when the Lord Jesus shall be revealed from heaven with his mighty angels in flaming fire taking vengeance on them that know not God, and that obey not the gospel of our Lord Jesus Christ."* (2 Thes. 1:6-8).

When it comes to tribulation to the troublers of our lives and our nation, it seems some of us are more righteous than God and we do not like to pray such prayers. But we have cases in the New Testament where God promises to judge the wicked troubling His elect. Luke 18:1-8 is a clear case. Like all other prayers, God determines how and when to answer our prayers in bringing judgment upon our troublers and enemies. Jesus said, "Shall not God avenge His own elect, which cry day and night unto him, *though he bears long* with them? I tell you that He will avenge them *speedily* ..."(Luke 18:7-8).

So, when we are living righteously but suffering tribulation from the wicked, either as a person, family or church or a nation and we continue to cry day and night unto God for God's judgment, it is Scriptural and righteous. God determines when and how He answers. But He expects us to cry unto Him day and night, otherwise, we continue to suffer. That is my understanding of Luke 18:1-8).

Yes, we are supposed to pray FOR the wicked and the enemy and feed the wicked when he is hungry, clothe him when he is naked. But the Bible says God converts such prayers and good works as "coals of fire" upon the head of the wicked (Romans 12:20). We are not supposed to avenge, but to pray. When you pray nice prayers for the wicked and God sees that the person does not deserve what you are praying for him or her, God will convert the prayers to fire upon his head. God determines how to handle such prayers.

Left for us as human beings, our enemies should die immediately, but God doesn't operate like that. He determines when and how to handle our foes. But He does not expect us to be suffering and be silent. Rev John Zechariah (the Baptist) was beheaded and his head given out as a trophy to a witch. Nothing happened. Apostle James was beheaded and nothing happened. Apostle Peter was arrested and was facing execution and the church rose up. Peter was delivered. A short while afterward, Herod was smitten by an angel and was eaten up alive by worms. His cup of wrath was full. If we don't pray, we become preys to our troublers.

#1. Worship God for His greatness.

#2. Song: Arise, O Lord, let Your enemies be scattered. 3x. O Lord, O Lord, arise!

#3. O God Almighty, be not silent about the wickedness in our land.

#4. Be not silent, O God, about the troubles of the righteous and the innocent in our land.

#5. Arise, O Lord, and begin to execute Your righteous judgment upon the wicked.

#6. There are people who are merchants of human parts in our land, drinkers of human blood and eaters of human flesh who are walking around with impunity. Arise, O God, and begin to exercise Your righteous judgment upon them.

Human beings have become a big business – slave trade, kidnapping for rituals, kidnapping for huge ransoms, kidnapping of young women by Islamic terrorists as sex slaves and for huge financial ransoms. Aborted babies are used for industrial use – for money. Babies are bred and harvested for sale to ritualists.

#6. O God, arise, let not evil continue to prevail in our lands.

#7. As there are earthquakes in some nations, O God, begin to shake the foundations of wickedness in our nation. Shake the foundations and hideouts of terror and occultism in our land.

#8. For defiling the land with human blood, let the earth begin to fight them.

#9. Let all the contractors and priests of wickedness begin to suffer tribulations.

Killing and kidnapping by Fulani herders Islamic terror groups in Africa continue. Newspapers are tired of reporting because this is no longer newsworthy except where the number is great.

But the word of God says, *"...but he that troubleth you shall bear his judgment, whosoever he may be..."* (Gal 5:10-12).

#10. Let heaven begin to trouble our troublers.

#11. We pray for rest for those who live in the troubled zones. Many cannot sleep because there may be an invasion any time in the night and there may be no intervention from soldiers or police until after the evil men have finished their works and gone

#12. Lord, command Your peace upon our nation.

#13. Father of the fatherless, please, comfort and raise help for the thousands of the fatherless, thousands of widows and all the bereaved in the nations.

#14. Heal all those who are in pains. Raise those who are battling to survive.

#15. We pray for all those who are still in the hands of their captors. Father, release them, in the name of Jesus.

#16. Let's praise the Lord for He is mightier than the mighty and is able to handle the wicked.

Prayer Session #49

THE BLESSING OF AN EVER-A-LOVER

1 Kings 5:1-6

1. And Hiram king of Tyre sent his servants unto Solomon; for he had heard that they had anointed him king in the room of his father: for Hiram was EVER A LOVER OF DAVID.

2. And Solomon sent to Hiram, saying,

3. "Thou knowest how that David my father could not build a house for the name of Jehovah his God for the wars which were about him on every side, until Jehovah put them under the soles of his feet.

4. "But now Jehovah my God hath given me rest on every side; there is neither adversary, nor evil occurrence."

5. "And, behold, I purpose to build a house for the name of Jehovah my God, as Jehovah spake unto David my father, saying, Thy son, whom I will set upon thy throne in thy room, he shall build the house for my name."

6."Now therefore command thou that they cut me cedar-trees out of Lebanon; and my servants shall be with thy servants; and I will give thee hire for thy servants according to all that thou shalt say: for thou knowest that there is not among us any that knoweth how to cut timber like unto the Sidonians."

Hiram was "ever a lover" till the death of David. He continued his love for David even after the latter's death. Solomon continued to enjoy Hiram's love for David. The love didn't expire even at the death of David.

Some people cannot maintain a relationship for a long time. Something 'genuine' always happens to justify the break-up or fight or separation. Some cannot maintain church membership.

Some don't have any problem getting new friends and lovers. But somehow, they disagree on some issues and they become irreconcilable out of bitterness and regret.

Some cannot maintain or retain customers or clients. Some people cannot retain relationship, friendship or clients or customers because of their attitude or behavior.

But for some people, regular losses of relationships can be spiritual. There are spirits that keep away good friends and good relationships and clients. I have known of couples who started physical fighting from the very night of their wedding. Some couples separate days, weeks, months or a few years after. Some separate after 30 years.

David enjoyed strong inseparable love from some people. First, from Prince Jonathan, Saul's son. Then from 30 mighty men who became his bodyguards and security details throughout his travails in the wilderness. None of them ever left him. When he was too weak to fight and the enemy almost cut him to pieces, they defended him. When he greatly desired water from the well of Bethlehem, his village, three of these men risked their lives to break through the garrison of Philistines soldiers to fetch the water.

Some helpers come at the nick of time or at strategic times to help. Some come only once in a life time. We need all.

But today, we are praying specifically for forever-lovers. A forever lover is a person who loves you in spite of your faults. He or she has a mandate on his or her spirit he/she must not betray you or leave you for someone else.

#1. Jehovah, God, I worship You that such facilities are still available for God's children.

#2. Lord, give me an ever-lover.

#4. Give me grace to enjoy forever-customers and clients.

#5. Father, I repent of any of my behaviors and attitudes that have made me lose good relationships you brought into my life.

#6. I reject rejection. In the name of Jesus Christ, my life will no longer experience rejection.

#7. My spouse's s love and respect for me will not expire.

#8. The respect, honor and admiration people have for me at the moment will not expire.

#9. The love of my benefactors will not expire.

#10. Father, give me the grace not to take people's love and honor for me for granted.

#11. Lord, make me an ever-lover too. Give me an unusual grace to bear with people.

#12. Father, redeem for me all my benefactors I have lost by my foolishness or behavior. (Please pray this prayer very well.)

When Hiram heard that David's son was made King, he personally sent to him and requested for his permission to help him. Solomon did not solicit for this help. His love for Solomon was unsolicited. It was a transferred love. He inherited an ever-lover. Some of us have suffered from transferred hatred. We inherited the enemies of our parents.

Solomon had a ministry project, a massive construction work that no engineer in Israel could handle, a majestic Temple. Hiram was ready to help.

#13. I prophesy to you: God will give you an enthusiastic helper from outside your domain – in the name of Jesus.

DELIVERANCE FROM OPPRESSIVE SLEEP

Genesis: 15: 11-12.

> *11. And when the fowls came down upon the carcasses, Abram drove them away.*
>
> *12. And when the sun was going down, a deep sleep fell upon Abram; and, lo, an horror of great darkness fell upon him.*

God created sleep for rest and to renew our health, especially, the functions of the organs of our body. Some organs like kidney do their works properly when we are sleeping. Also, when we are asleep, our spirits are also more active to receive information from the spirit realm.

However, it is also in sleep that most spiritual attacks are experienced. Many times, the enemies wait for us to sleep so they can launch an attack. Sometimes, an enemy may actually induce a sleep for the purpose of launching an arrow. Yes, not all sleeps are natural.

The enemy may drag you into the battle ground to deal with you through an imposed or forced sleep.

I know a lady who would always have vigils of prayer because since she got married, she had been facing serious attacks of eating in dreams. Someone would always give her food to eat.

This was serving as contraceptives to prevent or destroy her pregnancy. Because of this constant oppression, she would refuse to sleep but pray all night. However, in the day, while doing her normal work, she may sense a strange wind blowing on her face and she would doze off for a split second. And someone would put something into her mouth and she would wake up - just within a split second.

Another person said he would be forced to sleep every 2 hours and be given food to eat every time. No matter where he is and what he is doing, once the programmed time is up, he would sleep off immediately.

He used everything he knew to stay awake, even putting a peppery substance in the eyes, but nothing could stop this oppressive sleep.

Today, the Lord will deliver you from oppressive sleep - in the name of Jesus!

In our passage, we see Abraham just had a discussion with God. Then he made some sacrifices as demanded by God. But some birds came to eat the sacrifice of Abraham. Abraham didn't permit those birds to touch his sacrifice.

However, the next thing is: *"a deep sleep of great horror fell upon him."* This is not a normal sleep. And this wasn't a night. It was "when the sun was going down." The sun was just about to set, maybe around 6.30pm. What kind of sleep is that?

The Amplified Bible Classic Edition puts it this way:

> *11. And when the birds of prey swooped down upon the carcasses, Abram drove them away.*
>
> *12 When the sun was setting, a deep sleep overcame Abram, and a horror (a terror, a shuddering fear) of great darkness assailed and oppressed him.*

Here we can see this was no ordinary sleep.

God just gave Abraham some juicy promises and asked him to make a sacrifice to seal and activate the promises. But the moment he made the sacrifices to God, certain "fowls came down upon the carcasses" meant for God.

Have certain birds been eating your seed, your sacrifices? You give offering, give special sacrificial offerings and pledges, and your finances are still under attack.

Some of us may be giving to wrong preachers and wrong causes or feeding someone's covetousness. But some have made genuine sacrifices to genuine causes and nothing came out of it.

Could it be that certain fowls are coming down upon your sacrifices? What do you do to such birds? Abraham didn't kill them. He only sent them away.

Living Bible translation says:

> *And when the vultures came down upon the carcasses, Abram shooed them away.*

Then he came under an oppressive sleep.

You cannot just "shoo away" satanic vultures. If you don't seriously deal with certain birds who are interested in your sacrifices, your ministry, your money, etc, and you only send them away with a wave of hand and a "shoo" from your mouth, they may come back in the night to retaliate.

If you resist the spiritual vultures without fire upon your tongue, it would just amount to just a shoo or shhhhh.

#1. In the name of Jesus Christ, I receive fire upon my tongue. I take my authority under God Almighty, and I command: Every fowl eating my sacrifices, fall down and die!

#2. Every satanic bird eating my seed, fall down and die - in the name of Jesus! (If you are a business man whose finances have nosedived despite all your efforts and sacrifices, pray this very well. If you are a man or woman experiencing delay in child bearing, there may be some fowls eating your seed.)

Please pray this prayer very seriously tonight. Notice your dream afterward. There may be a reaction in the spirit realm.

If you are in Africa or some parts of Asia, you may observe that once a while near your shop, an unknown person deliberately scatters some grains of corn or millets in front of your shop. You see certain birds coming to eat the grains. This is not normal.

Such things are done by your competitors to eat away your sweat and sacrifices of labor. Your clients will be diverted to your competitor's shops. This is real. If you don't deal with this you would soon be out of that business.

#3. In the name of Jesus, every bird that has been commissioned from the kingdom of darkness against my finances, die!

#4. Father, deliver me from every oppressive sleep - in the name of Jesus.

#5. Every power waiting for me to sleep to attack me, I am no longer your victim.

#6. I shall no longer be powerless in my dream.

#7. I receive the power of the Holy Spirit, the power of an overcomer in the dream.

#8. O my spirit, receive a new strength and fire to defeat my enemies even while I am asleep.

#9. My spirit will not sleep and be helpless. I shall be awake and powerful while my body is at rest.

#10. Whatever evil that has been planted into my body while I am asleep, O God, flush them out of my body - in the name of Jesus.

#11. Every satanic sedative working in my body to make me sleep a sleep of oppression at certain times, expire today and be flushed out of my body - in the name of Jesus!

#12. From today, I shall be the winner, the overcomer and the oppressor in the dream. No longer shall I be a helpless victim in the dream. I give God praise.

Prayer Session #51

THE SECRET ANGUISH OF A MAN OF FAITH

Genesis: 15. 1-3

1. After these things the word of the LORD came unto Abram in a vision, saying, Fear not, Abram: I am thy shield, and thy exceeding great reward.

2. And Abram said, Lord GOD, what wilt thou give me, seeing I go childless, and the steward of my house is this Eliezer of Damascus?

3. And Abram said, Behold, to me thou hast given no seed: and, lo, one born in my house is mine heir.

Good and righteous people also have their secret personal anguish and challenges. Financially wealthy people also have their problems that their admirers do not know about. Outwardly, Abram seemed not to have any problem. He had much wealth and maybe thousands of servants or members of staff. With up to 318 strong men he trained as fighters for his personal and business security, his estate must have been like a whole village. So strong were these personal security men that they could defeat 3-4 kings and their national armies.

God assured Abram He would remain his 'shield' and exceeding great wealth.

But there was anguish in the heart of Abram. He expressed this, "...I go childless..."

People only admired his wealth and security; they never knew the pains in his heart that he could express only in God's presence.

#1. Father, I thank You for what people are admiring in my life. I give You all the glory for this.

#2. No matter what I am passing through in life, Lord, I know there are certain people who admire Your grace and gifts in one area of my life or the other. I thank You for this, Lord.

#3. But Lord, you know the secret anguish of my heart. You know the secret tears of my life. You know what the public do not know about my life. Father, settle me this year - in the name of Jesus!

4. Lord, give me a publishable testimony.

Since he had no child and was now over 75 years, Abram was probably already making an alternative will or plan of inheritance for his great wealth. He told God, " ...*seeing I go childless, and the steward of my house is this Eliezer of Damascus... to me thou hast given no seed: and, lo, one born in my house is mine heir.*"

God said, No. The will you wrote, giving all your wealth to your servant, is hereby cancelled. You will have your own son to inherit your wealth.

#4. Father, In the name of Jesus, I withdraw any alternative plan I have made against Your purpose concerning my life.

#5. Only Your perfect will shall be established in my life.

#6. I repent of my unbelief for not wanting to wait any longer.

#7. Abram cried to God, "Lord GOD, what wilt thou give me, seeing I go childless…" O my God, what will you give me as my days on earth are rolling on?

#8. As the Lord assured Abram "I am your shield", so I declare that the God of Abram is my shield. He is the shield of all the children of God in this nation and in the nations of the world.

#9. The Lord is our shield as the Church of Jesus Christ in Islamic, communist and Hindu lands. The enemy shall not prevail against the Church.

#10. Whatever the enemy has planned and waiting for an opportune time to execute, they will wait in vain.

#11. We declare that Jesus is Lord over our land.

#12. We praise Him for His might and glory.

Prayer Session #52

I WILL NOT HEAR EVIL

1 Samuel: 4. 10-21.

10. And the Philistines fought, and Israel was smitten, and they fled every man into his tent: and there was a very great slaughter; for there fell of Israel thirty thousand footmen.

11. And the ark of God was taken; and the two sons of Eli, Hophni and Phinehas, were slain.

12. And there ran a man of Benjamin out of the army, and came to Shiloh the same day with his clothes rent, and with earth upon his head.

13. And when he came, lo, Eli sat upon a seat by the wayside watching: for his heart trembled for the ark of God. And when the man came into the city, and told it, **all the city cried out***.*

14. And when Eli heard the noise of the crying, he said, What meaneth the noise of this tumult? And the man came in hastily, and told Eli.

15. Now Eli was ninety and eight years old; and his eyes were dim, that he could not see.

16. And the man said unto Eli, I am he that came out of the army, and I fled to day out of the army. And he said, What is there done, my son?

17. And the messenger answered and said, Israel is fled before the Philistines, and there hath been also a great slaughter among the people, and thy two sons also, Hophni and Phinehas, are dead, and the ark of God is taken.

18. And it came to pass, <u>when he made mention of the ark</u> of God, that he fell from off the seat backward by the side of the gate, and his neck brake, and he died: for he was an old man, and heavy. *And he had judged Israel forty years.*

19. And his daughter in law, Phinehas' wife, was with child, near to be delivered: and <u>when she heard the tidings</u> that the ark of God was taken, and that her father in law and her husband were dead, she bowed herself and travailed; for her pains came upon her.

20. And about the time of her death the women that stood by her said unto her, Fear not; for thou hast born a son. But she answered not, neither did she regard it.

21. And she named the child I-chabod, saying, The glory is departed from Israel: because the ark of God was taken, and because of her father in law and her husband. -

#1. I worship the Almighty God, Jehovah Shalom, for His mercy and peace I have long enjoyed. I refuse to take His grace for granted.

#2. I declare today that every evil plan the enemy has organized for any of my loved ones this year will fail - in the name of Jesus.

Words can break or build. Good news can excite and bad news can break a man. Information can affect the chemistry and physiology of the body. Through words, certain hormones can be released into the body that will cause either good feelings or damages to the body.

Prophet Eli heard a very bad news and fell down backward from a chair, his neck broke and he died.

#3. In the name of Jesus, I will not hear evil this year. My people will not hear evil news concerning me.

#4. No news or circumstance will break me this year - in the name of Jesus.

#5. The Philistines of this nation will not prevail over the people of God. The Philistines who have a program and project to overrun our nation with great slaughter and to take over the nation and hand it over to their god will not succeed.

#6. All their plans of great slaughter will fail. The Lord shall arise on behalf of the nation and deliver us from these evil men.

> *"...And when the man came into the city, and told it, all the city cried out."*

A number of our cities and villages in Africa have been crying out by the onslaught of Muslim jihadists.

#7. In the name of Jesus, our cities will no longer be crying out.

#8. Father, let the cries of our cities come to a permanent end - in the name of Jesus.

#9. In the name of Jesus, I cancel all the tears the devil has planned for me and my family this year. They shall not stand; neither shall they come to pass.

Hearing evil may increase blood pressure and in some extreme cases, someone may suffer stroke. The same bad news that killed Eli is the one that affected Mrs Phinehas, his daughter-in-law. Her emotional trauma led her into forced labor. It wasn't yet time for her delivery. But the bad news scattered her systems and physiology. The evil news probably released large amount of certain hormones like oxytocin into her body and contraction started immediately. The baby too might have felt the effect of this and wanted to come out by force.

When birth is induced or forced, it is always very, very painful. So, eventually, the woman gave birth to I-chabod, 'Glory-departed' and the woman also died. Bad news. Multiple tragedies on the same day!

#10. I reject any bad news that is capable of scattering my life.

#11. The Ark of God was stolen, the General Overseer of the Temple died, the two pastors of the Temple died, the family ministry terminated and ended permanently. Judgmental prophecy was fulfilled over the family.

#12. In the name of Jesus, glory will not depart from my family.

#13. My family will not experience desolation.

#14. Glory will not depart from the church of God in our nation.

#15. I will not be a victim of any tragedy or any evil circumstance this year - in the name of Jesus.

#16. I will not fall into the trap of the enemy - in the name of Jesus.

#17. I receive baptism of joy and peace in the Holy Ghost.

#18. Eli fell and died by bad news because he was "an old man, and heavy." We don't have to be "heavy" because of old age.

'Heavy' means Eli could not lift himself up again. He could not raise his hands or legs easily again. He was probably carried to the seat. Heaviness is by sickness. One of our elders in church is in his mid-80s. He drives himself and leads the hymnal choir in our church every Sunday. He is old but not heavy.

#19. In the name of Jesus, I will be old, and yet not be heavy. I will be old and will not be blind. I will be old and not be hypertensive, diabetic or have stroke.

#20. No sickness shall weigh me down.

#21. In the name of Jesus, I will not be on wheel chairs.

#22. My old age shall not be a regrettable period for me.

#22. I will not know pains and afflictions in old age.

#23. I shall not be oppressed physically or spiritually.

#24. I reject any heaviness in my spirit. I receive new life and revival in my body and in my spirit. No power shall weigh me down - in the name of Jesus.

Some African elders have a saying that one must have to make a choice between living long on earth and seeing evil.

We reject this - in the name of Jesus. As children of God these choices are not mutually exclusive. Living long is not an alternative to seeing or hearing evil.

#25. I will live long and my eyes will not see evil.

#26. Eli lived for 98 years and his eyes saw evil and his ears heard evil. That will not be my portion. I will fulfill my days. I will fulfill my years. Yet, I will not see evil. I will not hear evil. I will not live in regrets in my old age. I shall be alive to see all my children succeed.

#27. Eli lost the only two sons that should have succeeded him. The whole family and ministry perished on the same day!

#28. I will not lose any of my children. I will not weep over any of them – in the name of Jesus.

#29. We will not lose any of our pregnant women or any baby at birth. (If you know any pregnant woman in your church or neighborhood, lift her up in prayer).

Prayer Session #53

LORD, HEAL ME!

James: 5. 13-15

> *13. Is any among you afflicted? let him pray. Is any merry? Let him sing psalms.*
>
> *14. Is any sick among you? Let him call for the elders of the church; and let them pray over him, anointing him with oil in the name of the Lord:*
>
> *15. And the prayer of faith shall save the sick, and the Lord shall raise him up; and if he have committed sins, they shall be forgiven him.*

The three questions by James show that even though by the stripes of Jesus we were healed and we have facilities in the Kingdom for perfect health, yet we know that there are times when we experience affliction and sickness. I have seen in children of God several kinds of afflictions and sicknesses that cannot even be diagnosed or treated by medication or surgery. For some that can be treated, there may be no money to do all that is necessary. And some people die because of this. Where there is money, there may be wrong administration, human error or demonic manipulation in surgery and the sick may eventually die. We have lost quite a number of God's children to breast and prostate cancers, stroke, diabetes, heart failures, surgical complications, etc.

"Is any sick among you? Let him pray." Yes, indeed, many are sick among us: hypertensive, asthmatic and diabetic. Some of us are with arthritis, glaucoma and other eye problems, cancer, problems with brain, liver, heart, kidneys, skin, infertility, regular miscarriages, bone problems, sickle cell anemia, inexplicable pains, etc. Many of these sicknesses can go by better nutrition, herbs, correct medication, change of lifestyle, etc.

However, we all know that there are afflictions and sicknesses that will not just simply respond to such. In such cases, it is either there must be a divine intervention or the person continues to suffer or on the way to the grave. In the name of Jesus, this sickness will not take me to the grave.

"Is any merry? Let him sing psalms."

#1. Lord, baptize me with the Spirit of joy.

(Sing psalms - written biblical psalms, personal psalms, published hymns and choruses.)

#2. Father, let all the organs of my body praise You. Let there be no turbulence in my systems.

#3. My Father, in the name of Jesus, let me not know affliction and pain again.

#4. Lord, I plead for Your mercy for all Your children being afflicted among us in church and among my friends and relatives: Intervene in their cases and deliver them. (Mention some by name.)

#5. Father, deliver me from distress and hardships in life.

#6. I will not experience pain - in the name of Jesus.

#7. I will not know what is called cancer by experience. (Speak to every organ of your body and covenant it to God and forbid pain in any of it).

#8. Lord, I ask that all Your children being afflicted with cancer, let there be divine intervention. Let the process of destruction going on in their bodies ne reversed now - in the name of Jesus!

#9. Lord, if there is any disease in my body that is waiting for full blown manifestation, let it die in the name of Jesus.

#10. I will not die in afflictions. I will not die in any pain - in the name of Jesus.

#11. I will not expire untimely.

#12. I will fulfill my days in peace and in joy.

"Is any merry, let him sing psalms."

#13. My life shall be a life of merry and singing.

#14. Holy Spirit, instead of any oppressive sleep, put a song in my spirit every morning.

#15. Before the end of this month, give me a testimony that will inspire me into dancing.

I SHALL NOT BE A VICTIM OF HUMAN ERROR

Text: Psalm 3: 3.

> *But thou, O LORD, art a shield for me; my glory,*
> *and the lifter up of mine head.*

I went to a hospital to see a sister who just underwent surgery. A doctor had given her a post-surgery injection that made her to be having excruciating pains. She screamed throughout the night.

The nurses wanted to give her a second dose of the injection and she refused even though she didn't know the connection between the injection and her pains and also because her body wasn't stable to receive an injection.

When the doctor arrived in the morning, and saw the state of the patient, he was bothered and asked if the lady had stomach ulcer. She said yes.

"Ah! Why didn't you tell me you had ulcer? I wouldn't have given you that particular injection. If you had received the second one, you would have died by now!"

How would a doctor who is worth his name administer such an injection or any medication at all without finding out any available medical history of the patient or some necessary information? How would you administer a medication that you know can be lethal under certain circumstances without finding out the health condition of the patient? If this lady had died, the doctor would not have confessed his error. Nobody would know what has happened. Other doctors who find out the cause of death would never report it.

If you are living in a country where the government and society place high value on human life, maybe this prayer won't be relevant to you. But in my part of the world, many thousands have been killed and are being killed by their doctors and nurses through such human errors and no punishment goes with this. I have long desired to have an NGO to fight by litigation and massive embarrassing media campaigns against these regular 'medical errors' and carelessness. As humans, we all make mistakes in our areas of specializations and some of the errors in hospitals are simply accidental. But it seems when people do not place much value on human life and where there are no sanctions, people do not make much efforts to guard against such error. Many cases are sheer carelessness.

Some years ago in this same hospital above, one of my precious sisters in church was admitted there. She had lost some pregnancies through miscarriages. Now she was pregnant again. Her doctor gave her a prescription and she took it to the pharmacy. The concerned pharmacist (who is a Christian lady) looked at the prescription and asked, "Sister, you don't want your baby?"

"What kind of question is that? I don't understand."

It was a divine intervention. Why should the pharmacist ask such a question when she is there to sell her medicines? The 'medication drug' was to waste the baby my sister had prayed and fasted for. This handsome boy that could have been destroyed by this doctor's prescription is already in his first year in the university as at the time of this writing.

In a popular university teaching hospital a few years ago, a boy who had herpetic whitlow on a finger was given a dose of formaldehyde (formalin) injection on the infected finger. (Formalin is a chemical used to embalm dead bodies). The boy's finger became dead and useless forever.

The doctor killed not just the herpes simplex virus of whitlow, he killed the whole finger! And that was the end. It was an error.

In the same university teaching hospital, a brother who was an accident victim was admitted and was in a coma for two weeks. One senior consultant who is also a pastor was passing through the man's bed and requested to see the patient's medical file. He was shocked to see the next injection they wanted to give the patient. He would have died immediately. That was a divine intervention. He was a bachelor. Today he has four beautiful children. All those children would have died in him.

There have been cases where surgical materials like cotton wool or even metal instruments were left inside a patient's body after surgeries. Many people have died not because of their sicknesses but by wrong diagnoses and wrong drug administration or wrong surgery or wrong surgical procedures.

There have been human errors in the process of child deliveries that have led to brain damages and other paralyses or mortality of babies or mothers. The only son of the late Dr John Edmund Haggai, founder of Haggai International, was a victim of this kind of error. I wept on the day Dr Haggai told us the story of how this happened. The doctor who was taking delivery of the boy was drunk and did permanent irreversible damages on the brain of Johnnie.

There have been many cases of police accidental discharge that resulted in the death of innocent people. In early January

2020, Iranian military in a furious attempt to punish America for killing its military leader, shot down a passenger plane that led to the killing of 176 innocent passengers and crew. They said it was an error. Those lives were wasted and families thrown into mourning – by a human error.

PLEASE, TAKE MUCH TIME TO PRAY THESE PRAYERS AND FORBID THESE IN YOUR LIFE FOREVER.

#1. In the name of the Lord Jesus Christ, the Son of the Living God, I shall not be a victim of any human error.

#2. My children, my spouse, none of my church members shall be a victim of human errors - in the name of Jesus.

Hundreds of thousands have died on our roads through accidents. Many thousands have had their bones broken and they became paralyzed for life. Many of these accidents are caused by errors of judgment or carelessness.

In a few cases, some of the errors may not just be human, but aided by a demonic manipulation.

#3. In the name of Jesus, I shall not be a victim of demonic manipulation of any doctor, nurse, drivers and a law-enforcement agent.

#4. I shall not be at any place at a wrong time.

#5. Wrong people shall never handle any issue that concerns my life.

#6. No agent of darkness and candidate of demonic manipulation shall handle any of my applications.

#7. I refuse any joker from the kingdom of darkness.

#8. The Lord will guide me continually and order my steps.

#9. I will not ask a wrong person for help. The Lord will orchestrate a help for me.

#10. I reject any alternative to the plan and purpose of God for my life this year - in the name of Jesus.

Exodus 33: 14.

> *"And he said, My presence shall go with thee, and I will give thee rest."*

#11. Lord, I praise Your Name and thank You that You will always be with me and not leave me alone to be controlled by the wills and actions of men.

THE ENEMY WILL NOT TOUCH MY SUBSTANCE - Part 1

Job: 1. 10-21.

10. Hast not thou made an hedge about him, and about his house, and about all that he hath on every side? Thou hast blessed the work of his hands, and his substance is increased in the land.

11. But put forth thine hand now, and touch all that he hath, and he will curse thee to thy face.

12. And the LORD said unto Satan, Behold, all that he hath is in thy power; only upon himself put not forth thine hand. So Satan went forth from the presence of the LORD.

13. And there was a day when his sons and his daughters were eating and drinking wine in their eldest brother's house:

14. And there came a messenger unto Job, and said, The oxen were plowing, and the asses feeding beside them:

15. And the Sabeans fell upon them, and took them away; yea, they have slain the servants with the edge of the sword; and I only am escaped alone to tell thee.

16. While he was yet speaking, there came also another, and said, The fire of God is fallen from heaven, and hath burned up the sheep, and the servants, and consumed them; and I only am escaped alone to tell thee.

17. While he was yet speaking, there came also another, and said, The Chaldeans made out three bands, and fell upon the camels, and have carried them away, yea, and slain the servants with the edge of the sword; and I only am escaped alone to tell thee.

18. While he was yet speaking, there came also another, and said, Thy sons and thy daughters were eating and drinking wine in their eldest brother's house:

19. And, behold, there came a great wind from the wilderness, and smote the four corners of the house, and it fell upon the young men, and they are dead; and I only am escaped alone to tell thee.

20. Then Job arose, and rent his mantle, and shaved his head, and fell down upon the ground, and worshipped,

21. And said, Naked came I out of my mother's womb, and naked shall I return thither: the LORD gave, and the LORD hath taken away; blessed be the name of the LORD."

When Satan told God, "Hast not thou made an hedge about him, and about his house, and about all that he hath on every side? Thou hast blessed the work of his hands, and his substance is increased in the land", you could hear the pains and anguish of envy and jealousy of Satan.

#1. In the name of Jesus Christ, whatever the enemy is angry about in my life, Father, secure it.

From the story above, it is clear that it is not all cases of robbery that are because of unemployment or bad government.

Sabeans and Chaldeans had always seen Job's farm and cattle, his tractors and haulage business. They never attacked these businesses *until* Satan inspired them to do so.

Some robbery attacks are sponsored from the kingdom of darkness as personal attacks to kill or bring down a man's finances.

Satan can sponsor fraudsters to defraud or scam a person to bring his finances down.

A man was convinced that a particular politician was going to be the savior and messiah his nation needed at that time. He was so convinced that he put in all his life savings and his entire retirement gratuity into politics - several millions earned in 35 years of service. He used this to organize the Support Group for this politician in his own state, hoping that when the election is won, he would recover his investment through contracts and other benefits from government. But after the victory of the party, the leadership of the party didn't recognize him for any benefit. He lost while his beneficiaries are living in opulence.

#2. I shall not suffer any loss this year.

#3. I will not be foolish.

#4. This year, I shall not be driven by wrong convictions that will sink me financially.

#5. I shall not embark on any unprofitable project that I will regret.

#6. I shall not be a victim of robbery attacks - in the name of Jesus.

#7. I shall not be a victim of fraudsters and scammers.

In all the attacks of Satan, someone would always come back and say, "I alone am escaped ..."

#8. Whatever evil that is planned for me or other people this year, we will escape - in the name of Jesus.

#9. I will escape robbery attacks.

#10. I will escape accidents of any kind.

#11. I will escape kidnapping traps.

#12. I will escape assassination snares - in the name of Jesus.

#13. I will escape terror attacks.

#14. I will escape strayed bullets.

#15. I will escape tragedies of human errors - in the name of Jesus.

Sabeans and Chaldeans had always been there and never stole anything from Job or killed any of his staff. But this time, Satan just employed them and brought this strange idea to steal and slaughter. The staff members of job's companies were just victims of satanic fury. They knew nothing of what was going on. They did not offend anybody. They didn't die because they were sinners or because of any family curse.

#16. I shall not be a victim of satanic fury.

Some robbers do not really intend or plan to kill. Sometimes, one of them may just 'feel like' wasting the life of their victim even though the person did not resist them, and even if they have taken everything in the house.

#17. I will not be an instrument of cruelty (Gen. 49:5).

Some husbands or wives kill their spouse in a few- minutes fits of anger before they come to their senses - after the irreversible damage is already done.

#18. I will not be a vessel for Satan or any evil spirit to achieve any of their purposes.

> *16. While he was yet speaking, there came also another, and said, "The fire of God is fallen from heaven, and hath burned up the sheep, and the servants, and consumed them; and I only am escaped alone to tell thee."*

It is not the fire of God. It is not everything that comes from the sky that is from God or from the Heaven of God. Satan also has his base in the air. He is the prince of the power of the air (Ephesians 2:2).

Satan said he walks (and works) not only to and fro in the earth, but also 'up and down' - That is, horizontally on earth, and also vertically - between the earth and the sky. That fire that came from the sky was from Satan's operational base in the sky. Yoruba people know there is something like *'iná ayé, iná òrun, etc'* - the fire of the world, the fire of 'heaven' or the sky.

#19. In the name of Jesus, the fire of the enemy will not burn me.

#20. The fire of the enemy will not touch my finances or my children or my spouse.

#21. Father, protect my interests all over the world.

> *18. While he was yet speaking, there came also another, and said, Thy sons and thy daughters*

228

were eating and drinking wine in their eldest brother's house:

19. And, behold, there came **a great wind from the wilderness,** *and smote the four corners of the house, and it fell upon the young men, and they are dead; and I only am escaped alone to tell thee.*

Satan fired Job from the sky and also attacked from the wilderness. The wind attacked the four corners of the house to bring down all the four walls on the occupants so that no one would escape.

But one person escaped – a servant!

#22. In the name of Jesus, from any angle the enemy comes against me or my children or finance this year, the enemy will fail. We will all escape – in the name of Jesus.

None of the children of Job escaped this attack.

#23. My children will not be trapped in any evil web.

#24. They will not be trapped in immorality or any evil of their generation - in the name of Jesus.

And Job said, "...Naked came I out of my mother's womb, and naked shall I return thither: ..."

Job did not die naked. God clothed him again, gave him ten children again and restored everything he lost. He died big, he died wealthy.

#25. I might have come naked, but I refuse to go naked.

#26. I will not die in shame.

#27. The Lord will clothe me in dignity and honor.

#28. I will not die poor.

#29. I will not die unsung.

#30. I will not leave my children in debts.

#31. I will not die in pains and agony.

#32. I worship the Lord because He is almighty.

#33. I worship Him because Satan will not write the last chapter of my life.

THE ENEMY SHALL NOT TOUCH MY SUBSTANCE - Part 2

Job 1:14-17

14. And there came a messenger unto Job, and said, The oxen were plowing, and the asses feeding beside them:

15. And the Sabeans fell upon them, and took them away; yea, they have slain the servants with the edge of the sword; and I only am escaped alone to tell thee.

*16. **While he was yet speaking**, there came also another, and said, The fire of God is fallen from heaven, and hath burned up the sheep, and the servants, and consumed them; and I only am escaped alone to tell thee.*

*17. **While he was yet speaking**, there came also another, and said, The Chaldeans made out three bands, and fell upon the camels, and have carried them away, yea, and slain the servants with the edge of the sword; and I only am escaped alone to tell thee.*

*18. **While he was yet speaking**, there came also another, and said, Thy sons and thy* *daughters were eating and drinking wine in their eldest brother's house:*

19. And, behold, there came a great wind from the wilderness, and smote the four corners of the house, and it fell upon the young men, and they are dead; and I only am escaped alone to tell thee.

Verse 16. "While he was yet speaking,..."

Verse 17. "While he was yet speaking..."

Verse 18: "While he was yet speaking..."

Someone came to bring bad news of very serious robbery attacks and total destruction of one of the major business ventures of Job.

As Chairman/MD of the company, Job was still thinking about how to express his grief when another staff member ran inside to report that the second largest company of Job had been totally wrecked by armed bandits and terrorists. All members of staff killed.

Job's grief was doubled and he was about to explode in tears when another staff member rushed in from the head office to say a strange fire descended from the sky and razed down the entire factory and consumed all staff except the one that escaped to report. The fire wasn't electrical, not gas, not stove, no human error involved. It simply came from the sky and consumed the entire factory and staff! And no insurance was in place!

Job was now about to break down when another man ran inside and fell to the ground to report that all the ten children were eating and celebrating in the estate and had been killed by a strange localized hurricane. According to the report, the hurricane came upon only one house, the very house where all the children were enjoying themselves. What a hurricane! It targeted only one building, did its havoc and stopped.

All these happened in just one day. One tragedy in a life time is enough to break a man or woman. But here Job had four different major tragedies on the same day.

All he had labored for in about 50 years were gone within 12 hours.

If the devil gets any permission from God to touch your substance, for just one day, that one day would be more than enough for him to bring you down to zero. All that a man acquired or labored to acquire for 50 years may be down in ruins within a week. The enemy can ground a person in a moment. It is actually easier and cheaper to destroy than to build. Job was grounded in just one day operations of Satan.

#1. Father, You will not give a moment to the enemy of my soul to vent his anger on me.

#2. Lord, do not permit the prince of darkness to test or prove his wickedness in my life.

(Take a good time to pray this).

Job received four messengers on the same day. All of them with very, very bad news.

#3. This year, I will not receive a messenger of bad news in my house - in the name of Jesus.

#4. Lord Jesus, I shall never receive evil 'visitors' - in the name of Jesus.

#5. Evil will not visit our city and community.

#6. By the power of the Lord of hosts, I lock the gates of my city and community against invaders - in the name of Jesus.

#7. No affliction I ever experienced in life will repeat itself in my life again.

#8. Father, compensate me for every attack I have ever experienced.

#9. In the name of Jesus, the enemy will not break me.

> *Then Job arose, and rent his mantle, and shaved his head, and fell down upon the ground, and worshipped. (Job: 1. 20).*

"After all these tragedies, Job arose ... and worshipped."

This does not seem to make sense. Job worshipped!

A song says, "It will all end in laughter, the things the world expects to generate tears in me, it will eventually end in laughter."

#10. Every power that is sponsoring evil against my life, expire!

THE ENEMY SHALL NOT TOUCH MY SUBSTANCE - Part 3

Job 1: 18-19.

> *18. While he was yet speaking, there came also another, and said, Thy sons and thy daughters were eating and drinking wine in their eldest brother's house:*
>
> *19. And, behold, there came a great wind from the wilderness, and smote the four corners of the house, and it fell upon the young men, and they are dead; and I only am escaped alone to tell thee.*

In the above strange incident, a servant escaped, but ALL the ten children of Job perished.

A man traveling from Lagos to Ibadan in Nigeria arrived safely in Ibadan and got down at Molete to buy some loaves of bread. All his family members were inside the car. In less than 5 minutes, a tanker truck full of petrol lost control and fell and emptied its contents on this busy area with people on the road side selling wares with local kerosene lamps and those frying bean cakes. In a few seconds, the whole area was up in flames. Several people, shops and vehicles went up in roaring flames.

The fire caught up with the traveler's car with all his family members inside. In his desperation to rescue the family, he was caught up in the flames. The whole family perished in less than five minutes.

He had travelled more than an hour and had arrived Ibadan safely. In a few minutes, they would have arrived home. But the waiting for less than 5 minutes in a good place at a wrong time, and the whole family perished. If they had decided to eat something other than bread that night or buy the bread at Challenge Area, some three kilometers away where there were more bread sellers, the family would have escaped this tragedy.

A Nigerian travelling from Lagos to Benin City with all his family members pulled up beside the road to ease himself in a minute. He had barely started urinating when a truck came from behind and crushed the whole family and the car. All his children and wife perished. The car destroyed. He came home empty. He waited at a wrong place at a wrong time. He had a tragedy that was irreversible.

Another man who just had a promotion to a high post in a multinational oil and gas company was asked to come to him home town to receive a chieftaincy title. He went with his friends all his immediate family members. On their way back to Lagos, they had a multiple-vehicle accident and the man and all his family members perished with the brand new jeep he just bought for the chieftaincy honor.

#1. This year in the name of Jesus, I will not be in any place at a wrong time.

#2. My family will not be vulnerable to satanic attacks.

Job was protected. But the children were not. The children were always drinking, partying EVERY DAY. They were at a party when disaster struck.

Today the spirit in the air in our land is a drinking spirit. All our cities are becoming full of drinking clubs and pup houses.

#3. In the name of Jesus, the spirit of the age will not catch up with my children.

#4. I kill in them any appetite or admiration for a wrong lifestyle.

#5. My children shall not be vulnerable to the enemy.

#6. Satan was looking for an opportune time to strike the children of Job. He found the opportunity. They were drinking wine. In the name of Jesus, the forces waiting for any convenient time to strike my spouse or children will wait in vain.

The men who waited to buy bread or urinate did not do a wrong or sinful thing. They just made a quick decision that led to tragedies.

#7. I will not be at any place at a wrong time. I will not make a decision that will lead to regrets.

#8. Order my steps this year. Order the steps of my family members.

#9. We shall not be trapped by the enemy.

#10. We shall not wait at a wrong bus or train station of life.

#11. We bind the spirit of drunkenness taking over our cities and destroying our men and women - in the name of Jesus.

If you are living close to any of the drinking clubs, take evangelism more seriously. Also do some prophetic walks in the area and make some declarations and proclamations. Release the captives and ask God for the spirit of repentance.

Prayer Session #58

OVERTAKING THE OVERTAKER

Exodus 15:9:

> *"The enemy said, I will pursue, I will overtake, I will divide the spoil; my lust shall be satisfied upon them; I will draw my sword, my hand shall destroy them."*

Israel had served several Pharaohs for 430 years in cheap or even free labor and developed the economy and infrastructure of Egypt. But as Scripture says, Satan does not release his prisoners unless by force. He does not open the house of his prisoners (Isaiah 14:17).

When the enemy realizes you are free, don't think he would give up. His natural attitude is: "I will pursue ... and bring him back into my captivity. I will pursue and take back his blessings he has taken away...."

#1. In the name of Jesus, any pursuit of the wicked over my life and family this year shall be efforts in futility.

In this verse, the enemy had three "I will". These are his plans, his intentions, his projects.

#2. Any "I will..." of the enemy, any project, any proposal of the wicked over my life and family this month shall fail - in the name of Jesus.

#3. Any power that has pursued me from any point of my history to this time has come to the Red Sea of my life.

#4. I am crossing over to fulfil my destiny in greatness. Any stubborn pursuer following me will be buried this year.

When the enemy says, "I will pursue and overtake...", he is saying, "I will run faster than him or hcr and I will go ahead of him and block his way."

When the enemy overtakes, he goes ahead and frustrates your plans. He goes ahead to meet your benefactor to whisper to his ears to change his mind. He gets somewhere before you get there to misrepresent you. The man who has promised to help you suddenly changes his mind. He may ignore your calls or even block your number.

#5. In the name of Jesus, I overtake my overtaker. Every power that has gone ahead of me this year, hear the Word of the Lord: My Father is the Alpha and Omega. He has gone ahead of me to the end of the year and end of my life. He shall frustrate all my overtakers - in the name of Jesus.

#6. The Red Sea is the burial ground for those who attempted to overtake Israel to bring them back into captivity. This year shall be the Red Sea for the Pharaohs who have pursued me to this moment.

#7. The enemy says, "I will divide the spoil..." My blessing and divine allocation this year shall not be divided as spoils.

#8. My allocation shall not be given to others.

#9. I will receive in full my allocation for this year. The Lord will backdate all my blessings of the years past – in the name of Jesus.

Prayer Session #59

I SHALL GO BACK TO MY LAND OF DESTINY

Matthew 2:19-23.

19 But when Herod was dead, behold, an angel of the Lord appeareth in a dream to Joseph in Egypt,

20 Saying, Arise, and take the young child and his mother, and go into the land of Israel: for they are dead which sought the young child's life.

21 And he arose, and took the young child and his mother, and came into the land of Israel.

22 But when he heard that Archelaus did reign in Judaea in the room of his father Herod, he was afraid to go thither: notwithstanding, being warned of God in a dream, he turned aside into the parts of Galilee:

23 And he came and dwelt in a city called Nazareth: that it might be fulfilled which was spoken by the prophets, He shall be called a Nazarene.

It is a fact that some destinies may not be fulfilled unless some individuals die. That is just the reality we have seen in Scripture. Jesus, even as a Son of God, had to remain in Egypt till Herod died. So long as Herod was alive, Jesus would remain in 'exile' or remain a refugee in Africa.

Moses too was destined to lead Israel. But so long as all those who wanted to kill him were alive, he could not go back to Egypt to fulfill his destiny. Despite all his academic credentials according to Acts 7:22, Moses worked as a refugee for 40 years. Then God told Moses, "You can now go back to your country of nativity and fulfill your purpose because ALL the people who were seeking your life are dead." (Exodus 4:19).

It was not just the Pharaoh that knew about the case of Moses that was dead; the members of the aggrieved family were dead; all the prosecuting lawyers and the judge who insisted Moses must be repatriated from Midian to face criminal charges and justice were all dead.

In the same way, God told Joseph and Mary, "You can now go back home with the Holy Baby and fulfill destiny and other prophecies, because all those seeking the life of the boy are now dead".

He said ALL THEM that seek the life of the young child are dead. "...THEY are dead which sought the young child's life." (Mat. 2.20b).

"They" means it wasn't only Herod that was interested in eliminating Jesus. Herod had disciples; he had sympathizers, hired killers, party thugs and beneficiaries of the government who were ready to kill to preserve or perpetuate his throne. God made sure all of them were dead so that Jesus would return to fulfill destiny.

#1. All hands that are joined together internally and externally to kill the destiny of our nation, God will take care of them – in the name of Jesus.

#2. I declare that in the name of Jesus, my nation will fulfill her prophetic destiny.

#3. Every power that has kept me in financial exile, ministerial exile, professional exile, your time has expired over my life – in the name of Jesus.

#5. All power that has kept Christians in this country in political exile, your time has expired.

Even when Joseph returned home with Jesus, Achelaus, the son of Herod, had taken over power in place of his father. God knew that Achelaus was as dangerous as his father. He inherited not just the throne but the antichrist spirits in the former ruler.

#6. I decree that in the name of Jesus, all the Herods whose times have expired on the different thrones in my nation but who want their political sons to inherit their spirits and continue to rule as the former Herods, they shall be disgraced.

#7. All Achelauses who wish to continue the evil agenda of their political fathers will lose.

If Pharaoh and all those who had a case against Moses had not died, Moses could have died as a herdsman (a highly educated man who was "learned in all the wisdom of the Egyptians" - Acts 7:22).

#8. My learning shall not be in vain. The learning and intelligence of my children shall not be in vain – in the name of Jesus.

#9. I pray for our youths who have graduated for years and have nothing to do, that heaven will engage them in fruitful works.

#10. In the name of Jesus, I will not die or grow old in a wrong location.

With all that Moses read in school, he could not use his education until Pharaoh and all those seeking his life died. At 80 years in Midian, Moses could have died any time.

#11. I will not grow old or die doing a wrong thing.

#12. I will not die unfulfilled.

#13. In the name of Jesus, whatever have to die and whatever leadership have to change for me to fulfill my destiny, Father, let it happen.

#14. In the cases of Moses and Jesus, it was a change of government that made them to return from exile.

#15. Father, whatever change of government that have to take place in the land to bring me from exile, to bring our nation out of exile, let the change come – at all levels – in the name of Jesus.

Prayer Session #60

MY BLESSING AND BENEFITS SHALL NO LONGER BE DIVERTED

(1 Samuel 17:25-26; 18:17-21).

> *And David spake to the men that stood by him, saying, What shall be done to the man that killeth this Philistine, and taketh away the reproach from Israel? for who [is] this uncircumcised Philistine, that he should defy the armies of the living God?*
>
> *And the men of Israel said, '... the man who killeth him, the king will enrich him with great riches, and will give him his daughter, and make his father's house free in Israel.'*
>
> *"And Saul said to David, behold my elder daughter Merab, her will I give thee to wife: only be thou valiant for me, and fight the Lord's battle. ..."*
>
> *But it came to pass at the time when Merab, Saul's daughter should be given to David, that she was given to Adriel the Meholathite to wife...*
>
> *And Saul said, 'I will give him (Michal), that she may be a snare to him..."*

David didn't just volunteer to confront Goliath as a national service. Yes, he wanted to stop and remove this disgrace from Israel. But that was not the real reason he took the risk. There was a bargain about that risk he was about to take. He wanted a reward that would be worth the risk. He said, "What shall be given to the man that kills this man and removes this reproach from Israel?"

They said, the Goliath killer would be given "great riches" by the king. Secondly, the Goliath killer would be given the king's daughter to marry, and lastly, his family would have perpetual tax exemption.

Good deal.

I guess this wife offer was the tantalizing thing that excited this energetic bachelor.

However, the life of David shows us that killing the Goliath of your life does not mean you will automatically enter into all the benefits of such warfare immediately. David killed Goliath but didn't really enjoy the personal benefits he expected from this achievement. The king indeed promised "great riches". But we can't see any record of any "great riches" given him by King Saul.

The second reward expected was the king's daughter. King Saul had two daughters – Merab and Michal. His intention was to give the first daughter, the real lady he had in mind as an honor and reward to the Goliath killer. But after David killed Goliath, Saul changed his mind and gave Merab to another man, Adriel. Merab gave birth to 5 sons for this man (1 Samuel 18:17-21; 2 Samuel 21:8). Adriel did nothing to deserve Merab. Saul just 'dashed' her out free of charge to punish David for his new growing popularity in the nation.

However, someone told King Saul that his second daughter, Michal, was showing interest in David. King Saul was very happy. Why?

*"And Michal Saul's daughter loved David: and they told Saul, and the thing pleased him. And Saul said, I will give him her, **that she may be***

245

a snare to him, *and that the hand of the Philistines may be against him." (1 Sam 18:20-21).*

Saul probably knew that Michal was a bad girl. He was happy to give her to David, not as a gift and favor or generosity or reward for killing Goliath. The girl was to be given as a snare!

#1. O God, deliver me from every snare of the enemy!

Why wasn't he happy to give Merab to David as he had promised and wanted to do? I believe Merab was a choice girl, an excellent wife material, the dream lady of any man. She wasn't a snare, she wasn't a trouble maker. But Michal was probably known as a trouble maker and an abusive girl. Giving her to David was like a good riddance to bad rubbish!

To every blessing, promise or expectation, there are always alternatives. Those alternatives may bear the same name as the original. But they cannot fulfill the purpose of full satisfaction.

Having known Michal from childhood, the father knew this girl was a good candidate to be used as a trap to any young man Saul does not wish well.

What is a snare in marriage? A snare is a spouse you marry and after some time you ask yourself, "How did I get into this? Who blinded me? Was I under a spell? Did I not see this? Who advised me into this? I thought I prayed well. I thought I heard from God. God punish the prophet who saw vision for me to say 'the road was clear'! Why am I so unlucky to enter into this trap? Who will deliver me from this little hell fire?"

A snare is a spouse you are married to and later you wish to die than to continue in that marriage. You wish you had remained single or you wish you had waited a little longer before making that final decision.

It was a snare that Saul offered David. Even to marry this alternative, Saul said the 'dowry' would be 100 private parts of dangerous Philistines – the prepuce or foreskin (the fold of skin that covers the glans of an uncircumcised man's organ). In his zeal to 'manage' this alternative, David went out, fought valiantly and removed this prepuce from the private parts of 200 Philistines and submitted them to King Saul as 'dowry'!

What a dowry!

He most probably killed those men before removing their foreskins or left them bleeding. What wickedness! What would Saul do with 100-200 foreskins of people's private part?

Later we see this Michal abusing and disparaging King David when he was dancing to worship God. She was too dignified as a princess to dance before God. She became barren till she died. So David could have died childless if he had not married other women. Meanwhile, the real wife he was to marry gave birth to 5 sons for another man, Adriel.

Later, even this Michal, this alternative, for whom David fought and probably killed was taken from David and given to another man (1 Samuel 25:44):

> "But Saul had given Michal his daughter, David's wife, to Phalti the son of Laish, which [was] of Gallim."

This was the second girl that David risked his life to marry. He could have been killed. Here, even the alternative was taken away from him. Adriel and Phalti who married these two ladies were not said to have done anything to get the ladies; they were not even said to have paid any dowry.

In the name of Jesus Christ, and according to Isaiah 65:21-23:

247

#1. The rewards of my labor shall not be diverted to others.

#2. I shall build houses, and inhabit [them;]

#3. I shall plant vineyards, and eat the fruit of them.

#4. I shall not build, and another inhabit;

#5. I shall not plant, and another eat:

#6. For as the days of a tree so shall my days be,

#7. I am an elect of the Lord and I shall long enjoy the works of my hands.

#8. I shall not labor in vain, nor bring forth for trouble;

#9. For I am the seed of the blessed of the LORD, and my offspring with me.

#10. The Lord shall guide me continually.

#11. He shall satisfy my soul in drought and in general scarcity.

#12. He shall make fat my bones and make me like a watered garden and like a spring of water whose waters do not fail.

#13. The Lord will cause me to ride upon the high places of the earth and feed me with the heritage of Jacob (Isaiah 58:11,14).

For about thirteen years while David was roaming about from forest to forest, he was just picking women at random. It seems when someone is frustrated from the foundation of his life, many things will go awry. We never see David doing any proper wedding or marriage ceremony till he died. And even though he had a number of children (19 known sons and some daughters), many of them were bad boys – rapist, incestuous deceivers, killers, traitors, liars, etc! He had 9 wives and at least 10 known concubines. Foundation. Maybe if he had married his Merab, there would have been no need for all this harem and retinue of women around him.

After the death of King Saul, David sent a message to Saul's son who was now on the throne to look for his wife, Michal, and send her back to him immediately:

13. And he said (to Abner, Saul's Chief of Army Staff), Well; I will make a league with thee: but one thing I require of thee, that is, Thou shalt not see my face, except thou first bring Michal Saul's daughter, when thou comest to see my face.

14 And David sent messengers to Ish-bosheth Saul's son, saying, Deliver [me] my wife Michal, which I espoused to me for an hundred foreskins of the Philistines.

15 And Ish-bosheth sent, and took her from [her] husband, [even] from Phaltiel the son of Laish.

16 And her husband went with her along weeping behind her to Bahurim. (2 Samuel 3:13-16)

#14. In the name of Jesus Christ, I will not labor in vain.

#15. The reward of my labor that has been taken away or diverted, shall be reverted back to me.

#16. My promotion and legitimate entitlements shall not be given to others.

#17. All promises that have been hijacked and diverted from my life, I revert them back – in the name of Jesus.

#18. Every horn that is scattering my blessings, be frayed – in the name of Jesus.

#19. In the name of Jesus, I reject any alternative to the perfect will of God for my life.

#20. I reject any Satanic Michal prepared as a snare for me.

#21. My daughter will not marry a snare.

#22. My sons will not marry snares – in the name of Jesus.

#23. Any exchange that has been done in the spirit realm over my allocation, I revert it – in the name of Jesus.

#24. All power that is jealous of my success, Lord, disgrace them.

Because David experienced frustration and denial at the foundation of his matrimonial life, he never had a good marriage or home till he died. His marriages to Abigail, Bathsheba, were under questionable circumstances.

#25. Father, whatever has been wrong at the foundation of my matrimonial life, education, career, redeem it for me – in the name of Jesus.

David who was promised "great riches" if he could kill Goliath was later found in the forest begging for food from a farmer, Nabal, who refused and insulted him. (1 Samuel 25:3-14).

#26. I shall not beg for food; I shall not beg for anything. Let the anointing of the Lord upon me attract all the helps I need – in the name of Jesus.

ARROWS OF ARCHERS AND ANOINTING OF ASHER

Of Joseph, the Bible says, *"Archers sorely grieved him and shot at him and hated him."* (Genesis 49:23).

The hatred Joseph suffered was as if archers released arrows against him.

Today, there are many arrows "that flieth by day" and "pestilence walking in darkness" (Psalm 91:5-6).

#1. I shall not be a victim. My family members shall not be victims.

We have seen a number of children of God dying in the midst of their days, including preachers and or their wives or children. Some may be because of work and ministry stress; some may be because of wrong nutrition, some died for not doing medical tests regularly to know the state of their health early. But some have died by arrows of archers. Some archers are church members. This I know very well. If there were 'Jezebels' and 'her children' in the New testament church in Revelation 2: 20-23, then we cannot imagine we are so righteous and full of faith in our generation that there can be no evil people in good churches.

King Saul died through the arrows by the archers.

"And the battle went sore against Saul, and the archers hit him; and he was sore wounded of the archers" (1 Samuel 31:

Saul did not survive it.

He had defeated Philistines in many battles before. But this time, the arrows of the Philistine archers caught him.

#2. In the name of Jesus, the archers will not catch up with me.

#3. I will not fall before the enemies I once defeated.

#4. The powers that have not given up on me will not see my end – in the name of Jesus.

King Josiah was a righteous king, one of the greatest and righteous kings of Judah after David and Hezekiah. But the archers caught up with him one day when he took a wrong decision by helping a wrong man, following and defending a man who was destined to die on the battle ground.

"And archers shot at King Josiah..." (2 Chronicles 35:23).

He didn't survive it.

Righteous, but hit by the arrows of archers. He became Head of State at the age of 8 years. Even though his father, Amon, and his grandfather, Manasseh, were fanatical idol worshipers and occult members, yet this young boy never copied any of their evil behaviors. I don't know who discipled him. There was no single day this boy did wrong. He lived every day in the fear of the Lord. He heard how God dealt with his grandfather, Manasseh, because of idolatry. He heard about how God punished his own father for idolatry. He decided he won't follow the way of the fathers.

There was a prophecy over Josiah's life several years before he was born that he would be the one to cause revival in Judah and that he would arrest and cremate all the occult men in Judah. The national idolatry that Jeroboam started, he was to be the one to stop it (1 Kings 13:2).

In 2nd Chronicles 34:2, we read, *"And he did that which was right in the sight of the LORD & walked in the way of David his father, and declined [neither] to the right hand, nor to the left."*

Josiah caused a revival of righteousness that no king ever caused in Israel. The Passover he celebrated was the best ever after the time of Samuel. *"...while he was yet young, he began to seek after the God of David his father: and in the twelfth year he began to purge Judah and Jerusalem from the high places, and the groves, and the carved images, and the molten images. (34:4).*

"And they brake down the altars of Baalim in his presence; and the images, that [were] on high above them, he cut down; and the groves, and the carved images, and the molten images, he brake in pieces, and made dust [of them,] and strowed [it] upon the graves of them that had sacrificed unto them.

34:5. And he burnt the bones of the priests upon their altars, and cleansed Judah and Jerusalem."

Josiah combed all the forests of Judah where there were human rituals (that his grandfather started). He arrested all the priests in those forests and burnt them to ashes.

#5. O God, give us a Josiah in this land - to clear our forests of human part merchants and kidnappers.

Josiah did very well for all the 31 years he ruled. But just in one day, he made a decision that ruined him and terminated his life. Josiah didn't die because he was a sinner. He died because of wrong judgement, wrong decision. He was convinced that that decision was right. But he was wrong. He became vulnerable to archers. He died at the age of 39.

#6. Oh God! Have mercy on me. Let me never take a wrong decision that will give archers access into my life.

#7. Lord, I pray for all your children who might have been hit already by the archers. Lord, have mercy and deliver them. (Please, mention any child of God you know who may be under any affliction. Some of them are hit not because they are sinners or prayerless; some are hit because no one is covering them in prayers.)

If you are a pastor, ask the Lord to lead you to select a few people to be praying for you and your family regularly. Get another small prayer group that will be covering church members and also fish out archers in the church.

Joseph: Of Joseph, the Bible says, *"Archers sorely grieved him and shot at him and hated him."* (Genesis 49:23).

How did he overcome these "arrows"?

> "But his bow abode in strength and the arms of his hands were made strong by the hands of the mighty [God] of Jacob; (from thence [is] the shepherd, the stone of Israel:)
>
> 49:25. [Even] by the God of thy father, who shall help thee; and by the Almighty, who shall bless thee with blessings of heaven above, blessings of the deep that lieth under, blessings of the breasts, and of the womb:

Anointing simply is God helping a man to do what he needs to do that is beyond his natural ability. Joseph experienced arrows of archers, but his own spiritual bow received "strength by the hand of the Mighty God of Jacob.

#8. In the name of Jesus, I receive strength from the hand of the mighty God of Jacob.

#9. My bow shall abide in strength.

#10. My hands shall be strong by the hands of the mighty God.

#11. As Joseph, the Lord God of Israel shall bless me with the blessings from above and blessings of the deep that lie under.

#12. I receive blessings of the deep that lies under.

#13. For myself and my children, I receive "blessings of the breasts and of the womb."

Genesis 33:24-25:

> 24 *"And of Asher he said, 'Let Asher [be] blessed with children; let him be acceptable to his brethren, and let him dip his foot in oil.*
>
> 25 *Thy shoes [shall be] iron and brass; and as thy days, [so shall] thy strength be."*

#14. I receive the blessing of Asher upon my life and family. We receive shoes of iron and brass to thread upon archers.

#15. As my days, so shall my strength be.

#16. I shall dip my foot in the oil of nations.

#17. My feet shall be anointed

Prayer Session #62

I WILL NOT DIE AT THE KADESH OF MY DESTINY

(Numbers 20:1).

> *Then came the children of Israel, even the whole congregation, into the desert of Zin in the first month: and the people abode in Kadesh; and Miriam died there, and was buried there.*

Israel had left Egypt and already had spent 39 years in the wilderness. In the first month of the 40th year, Miriam died and was buried in Kadesh, just as they were entering the border of their Destiny Land.

We don't know what killed Mariam. But having been in the wilderness for 39 years, she died 11 months to her destination. Aaron also died in the same chapter. They had lived all their lives expecting to enter the promise and prophecy of "milk and honey" Canaan. They died at the border of their destination.

***

#1). In the name of Jesus, I will not die unfulfilled.

#2). I will not die at the Kadesh of destiny.

#3). I will not die at the Kadesh of ministry.

#4). I will not die at the border of my dream fulfillment.

What a privileged family! Miriam, Aaron and Moses - three distinguished and privileged members of the same family, leading a whole nation, yet all of them did not get to the Promised Land.

Theirs was a most favored family - the national Music Minister/Director, the National Priest and the National Prophet. But none of them got to the Promised Land!

***

#5). In the name of Jesus, I refuse any family limitation. What stopped others in my family will not stop me - in the name of Jesus!

***

Immediately they moved from Kadesh towards Canaan at Mount Hor, Aaron died. He died in the same chapter, the same year in the same family. He wasn't sick and he didn't have an accident. Even though he was old, he didn't die because of old age. God simply killed him. The family had not fully recovered from the death of Miriam, his sister, when he died.

***

#6). In Jesus name, evil will not visit my family this year. The mercy of the Lord will preserve every member of my family - in the name of Jesus.

***

Aaron died 4 months after his sister Miriam died. Numbers 33. 38 says:

> *"And Aaron the priest went up into mount Hor at the commandment of the LORD, and died*

there, in the 40th year after the children of
Israel were come out of the land of Egypt, in the
first day of the 5th month."

This was 7 months to the Promised Land. He had ministered for 39 years 5 months but ended badly 7 months to his rewards and celebrations.

***

#7). I will not lose my rewards - in the name of Jesus.

OH GOD, DO NOT REMOVE MY GARMENTS!

When the congregation had no water, God told Moses and Aaron:

> *"Take the rod, and gather thou the assembly together, thou, and Aaron thy brother, and speak ye unto the rock before their eyes; and it shall give forth his water, and thou shalt bring forth to them water out of the rock: so thou shalt give the congregation and their beasts drink." (Numbers: 20. 8).*

Later, we read:

> *22. And the children of Israel, even the whole congregation, journeyed from Kadesh, and came unto mount Hor.*

> *23. And the LORD spake unto Moses and Aaron in mount Hor, by the coast of the land of Edom, saying,*

> *24. Aaron shall be gathered unto his people: for he shall not enter into the land which I have given unto the children of Israel, because ye*

rebelled against my word at the water of Meribah.

25. Take Aaron and Eleazar his son, and bring them up unto mount Hor:

*26. And **strip Aaron of his garments**, and put them upon Eleazar his son: and Aaron shall be gathered unto his people, and shall die there.*

27. And Moses did as the LORD commanded: and they went up into mount Hor in the sight of all the congregation.

*28. **And Moses stripped Aaron of his garments, and put them upon Eleazar his son; and Aaron died** there in the top of the mount: and Moses and Eleazar came down from the mount.*

29. And when all the congregation saw that Aaron was dead, they mourned for Aaron thirty days, even all the house of Israel. (Numbers 20:22-29).

God told MOSES, "remove the garments of Aaron." The garments were what distinguished Aaron from about three million people. When he was to be given those garments, God explained the significance of these special garments.

> *"And thou shalt make holy garments for Aaron thy brother <u>for glory and for beauty</u> (Exodus 28:2).*

Aaron didn't buy or sew the garments. They were designed and customized for him by God's instruction. Bezaleel and Oholiab who designed and sewed the garments received special inspiration from God for this. They were not a design anyone else could copy or get in any market. The garments symbolized the ministerial glory and beauty God specially brought on Aaron. This was a former ordinary farmer, laborer and slave in Egypt.

But here God says in essence, 'remove his honor and dignity. Bring him to zero; bring him to the same level of everybody. Take away his ministry and put it on someone else!'

Lord, have mercy on me!

Aaron ended in shame; he ended disrobed of priestly robes in front of the congregation that had respected him as a great man of God who had been ministering directly with the General Overseer.

#1). Father, whatever dignity You have given me in life and ministry, let me not lose it.

#2). Whatever honor you have given me as Your son and minister, let me not lose it by any misbehavior.

***

Today, many people have lost their garments, their honor and dignity as ministers. But they still continue ministry as usual! They still have their own personal garments, their undies and even some expensive jackets. But God has removed His own garments.

As Aaron's garments were removed, the next thing was death. When God strips a man of his ministerial garments, it is better for him to ask the Lord to take him away to heaven immediately before he loses his soul. The ministry is over. The glory and beauty have departed. Whatever the man does after the garments are off, he is on his own. It is shame and disgrace that will characterize his life and 'ministry' thereafter. Such a person becomes an embarrassment to the kingdom of God. His 'ministry' will be abhorrent to people even if some people are still clapping for him. People can begin to backslide because of him. He will be a minus to the kingdom of God.

#3). In the name of Jesus, I shall not be disgraced. I shall not be an embarrassment to the people of God.

#4). Father, let Your grace sustain me. I shall not lose my dignity.

The whole congregation saw what happened to Aaron.

#5). O God, my Father, let me not suffer shame before those who respect me as God's servant.

***

When God was talking to Moses about the implications of striking the rock instead of speaking to it, He said that Aaron too would not enter the Promised Land because *"ye rebelled against My word at the water of Meribah."* (v.24).

It was Moses that struck the rock, not Aaron. But God said, 'ye' (plural). God held Aaron also responsible. Even though it was both of them that God gave the instruction to speak to the rock, it was Moses that struck the rock. But God punished Aaron also for this. Why?

If your leader does a thing that you know is a blatant disobedience to God and you keep quiet, you might be taken as an accomplice and share in the implications. In the wilderness, there were cases of family members who suffered death for what a father did - The families of Achan, Korah, Abiram, Dothan, etc.

WHEN THE ENEMY REMOVES THE GARMENTS

Sometimes, it may not be God that removes someone's garments. A person may be dreaming often of seeing himself naked in dreams, half naked or in rags or in dirty places. This is not a punishment from God, but an attack from the kingdom of darkness.

***

#6). In the name of Jesus, I shall not suffer shame. Lord, cover my nakedness.

#7). Whatever glory, honor and dignity has been taken out of my life in the spirit realm, I recover today, in the name of Jesus.

***

The garments of Aaron were given to Eleazar.

#8). My glory and honor will not be exchanged - in the name of Jesus.

#9). I thank You, Lord, for Your grace and facilities available today that Aaron may not have enjoyed.

#10). Aaron did not have an advantage of a second chance. I receive the grace of a second chance today, in the name of Jesus Christ.

Prayer Session #64

"SPEAK TO THE ROCK" - Part 1

In their journey in the wilderness after the death of Miriam, the people of Israel had no water and were upset with Moses. He and Aaron went to God to plead for His intervention. They had not even opened their mouths to pray when God spoke:

> 8. *"Take the rod, and gather thou the assembly together, thou, and Aaron thy brother, and speak ye unto the rock before their eyes; and it shall give forth his water, and thou shalt bring forth to them water out of the rock: so thou shalt give the congregation and their beasts drink.*
>
> 9. *And Moses took the rod from before the LORD, as he commanded him. ....*
>
> 11. *And Moses lifted up his hand, and with his rod he smote the rock twice: and the water came out abundantly, and the congregation drank, and their beasts also.*

***12.** And the LORD spake unto Moses and Aaron, Because ye believed me not, to sanctify me in the eyes of the children of Israel, therefore ye shall not bring this congregation into the land which I have given them. (Numbers: 20. 8-12)*

God said, "Take the rod... Speak to the rock..."

God didn't tell Moses and Aaron what to do with the rod. He only said take it. He didn't ask them to use it.

Also, God didn't speak here through a dream that could be misinterpreted or forgotten. It wasn't a vision that could be misunderstood. This was a clear audible voice of instruction and both of them heard the voice.

***

#1. Holy Spirit, give me grace to note details in Your instructions and dealings with me.

***

The rod was anointed, but it was not to be used on this occasion. The rod had been used for some other miracles in the past. It had even been used to bring out water from the rock sometime ago. But it is not the instrument to be used for this miracle water. Even though God asked him to hold the rod in his hand, He didn't say he should use it.

It is easy to idolize any object or substance God might have used to perform a miracle in my life and in the lives of others in the past. I need to be careful. God will not share His glory with anybody or with any object, even anointed objects.

Anything can become an idol or fetish: olive oil, water, handkerchiefs, holy rods or sticks, holy jackets, etc. God can and does use any of these things as points of contact to do miracles. He did that in the Bible and still does so today. God can use even palm oil to do miracles. (It is not the chemistry of olive oil that brings a miracle. It is the presence of the Lord upon a child of God.)

But nothing must distract people from their focus on God, the Miracle Worker.

From around early 1990s to this moment in the church in Africa and America, olive oil has suddenly become a big industry, a big business. Today we operate as if nothing can happen without olive oil and pieces of cloths.

Some of us do "anointing service" with olive oil every week or every month since the one of last week has 'expired' or dried up. And people rush for it (because we are fetish by nature and culture). We make people believe that they are not secure continually even under the grace of God unless they come regularly for this physical oil. We know our people like things added to prayers and we capitalize on this.

I know of an African preacher in UK some years ago showing on TV different types of "anointing oils" for different uses. The oil bottle for wealth is different from the one for husband attraction, and the ones for favor, promotion, headache, diabetes, hypertension, visa collection, immigration papers, etc. Each of them has its cost implications. Someone even produced customized handkerchiefs with his image and gave them to highest bidders. I know of a lady who paid £2,000 to get such handkerchief in order to get a husband. Yet no husband came after years.

Some pastors' jackets are 'auctioned' and taken over by the highest bidders because of the "anointed sweat" of the man of God on the jacket.

Some oils are taken from some special apostles and pastors and used to anoint those who can give certain amount of money for 'God's work'.

Some olive oils are brought from Jerusalem as special. Israel had probably sold more volume of olive oil in the past 30 years than it ever did in all her history. God will not spare idolatry in any form.

Many shameful things are being done today, especially, in the name of ministering deliverance.

***

#2. O God, have mercy on my generation for the shame we are bringing on Your name.

#3. Father, help me to keep my focus and hope in You and not in things or formulas.

#4. Only You are the source of real power and miracles.

#5. Lord, I believe in You and You only. I believe I carry Your invisible presence.

#6. I carry Your invisible oil upon me. Whoever I touch or pray for, let Your presence show forth - in the name of Jesus.

#7. I carry Your glory. Help me to live continually in this consciousness.

#8. It is You that work in me both to will and to do Your good pleasure (Phil 2:13).

#9. When people are healed, it is You and not me or things.

#10. When people are delivered, it is You and not me or any oil.

#11. I repent of all forms of idolatry in the church of which I am a partaker.

*#12. Holy Spirit, give me the consciousness of Your presence in my life all the time.

#13. Holy Spirit, help me not to grieve You by attracting people's attention to my dramatics and things as sources of miracles.

#14. Where I need to speak only, let me not strike or do any other thing.

***

God punished Moses because His instruction to him was very clear and unambiguous.

***

#15. Father, where I need to carry out specific instructions, let Your leading be very clear to me.

***

Maybe when Moses heard, "Take the rod ....speak to the rock...", he may not have paid attention to "speak" because he was already used to the ministry of the rod.

God regarded this as disobedience punishable by death! Ha!

***

#16. Oh God, help me to hear You clearly and pay attention to details!

#17. Let me not enter into any trouble by any presumption or assumption.

***

When Moses used the anointed rod, miracle happened. The water the congregation needed came out "abundantly" from the rock. They drank and were satisfied and praised the Lord. But God wasn't impressed. Yes, even though the congregation might have shouted hallelujah and clapped for Moses as a great man of God, God was angry and said, "ye believed me not."

Some things we do in public as an act of faith may be regarded by God as unbelief and may attract God's punishment sooner or later even when the things worked. A man can be guilty of 'ministry'!

***

#18. Lord, help me. Let me not be guilty of a wrong ministration.

***

God punished Moses for this. Even Aaron too was punished because he, as an elder brother and high priest, was there and didn't see anything wrong or draw the attention of Moses to the deviation from the divine instruction they both received.

It is easier and cheaper to get into trouble than to get out of it. It took less than three seconds to smite the rock twice. But that 3-second ministration disqualified Moses from entering the Promised Land after 40 years of ministry and suffering in the wilderness. If God so dealt with Moses, I need to be careful. God has not changed. He said, "I am the LORD, I change not."

***

#19. Oh Father of spirits, help me not to be hasty in my spirit to do or say anything I will live to regret.

***

This 3-second act of anger did not allow for repentance or forgiveness. Moses and Aaron didn't go to Hell fire, but they were punished. When Moses asked God to forgive him and allow him to enter the Promise, God refused (Deut. 3:23-27).

Aaron, on his own, did not even pray about it. God stripped him of his priesthood and retired him by death.

***

#20. Father, let me not do anything that would lead to irreversible punishment and implications.

***

Moses died in the 11th month of the 40th year - one month to cross over finally to the Promised Land! (Deut. 1:3. 33:45, 48-52).

***

#21. My God, let me not expire at the brink of my success journey.

#22. Lord, I avail myself of Your sustaining grace. I thank and praise You because I know You will keep and preserve me to the end.

***

23. Now unto him that is able to keep you from falling, and to present you faultless before the presence of his glory with exceeding joy, 25. To the only wise God our Savior, be glory and majesty, dominion and power, both now and ever. Amen. (Jude 23-24).

Prayer Session #65

SPEAK TO THE ROCK - 2

Numbers 20:8

God told Moses and Aaron:

> *"Take the rod, and gather thou the assembly together, thou, and Aaron thy brother, and speak ye unto the rock before their eyes; and IT shall give forth HIS water, and thou shalt bring forth to them water out of the rock: so thou shalt give the congregation and their beasts drink."*

From here, we can see that two pronouns are used for the rock – 'it' and 'his'.

Even though, naturally and scientifically, a rock is an 'it', yet spiritually, a rock can be a 'he'. In the New Testament, Paul says this Rock in the Wilderness was actually a 'he' (1 Corinth 10:4).

In prayer and prophetic actions, we can speak to things because they have 'ears' and can respond to the voice of their Maker, when we speak by the authority of their Maker.

This should not be construed as a form of animism. Animism is the belief that inanimate objects have souls or life and can be worshipped. That is the basis for idolatry. I am not teaching animism. But we have several examples of prayers going beyond the level of talking to God. Speaking to the rock or things does not mean making petition to things. But we see in Scripture that sometimes after talking with God, He may inspire us to speak to the situations or to speak to things.

For example, after Joshua spoke to the Lord about a battle he had to win before the end of the day, he went outside to speak to the sun and the moon:

> "Then spake Joshua _to the LORD_ in the day when the LORD delivered up the Amorites before the children of Israel, _and he said_ in the sight of Israel, _Sun, stand thou still_ upon Gibeon; _and thou, Moon,_ in the valley of Ajalon. 13. And the sun stood still, and the moon stayed, until the people had avenged themselves upon their enemies. Is not this written in the book of Jasher? So the sun stood still in the midst of heaven, and hasted not to go down about a whole day" (Joshua 10:12-13).

The whole solar system responded, the earth movement was suspended and the moon and sun remained in their positions until the battle was over. That is a high level of prophetic action that one cannot attempt presumptuously.

In secret, Jesus spoke to God in prayer. In public, He spoke to things and situations on a number of occasions. He spoke to the fig tree. He spoke to the sea, wind, storm, etc. He said we can speak to mountains; we can speak to mulberry trees to move.

It is the authority, mandate or faith we receive with God in the secret place that determines our effectiveness in speaking to things and situations.

Joshua spoke to God, then he faced the Sun and the Moon and spoke to them.

Moses and Aaron had been to God. Then God asked them to go out and "speak to the rock" in the presence of the congregation.

As we have seen in Scripture, the rock in the wilderness was both an 'it' and a 'he'.

God said as they simply speak, the rock would release "his water" to them. The rock had 'his' water.

***

#1. Give quality worship to the King of kings who has authority over all His creation.

#2. Lord, I ask that as the Rock of Ages, that you may release Your water to cool my life, hydrate every aspect of my life and satisfy every thirst of my life.

#3. You are the source of my joy, source of true love. Release your joy and peace into my body and my soul.

#4. Things as rock. Speak to situations of your life. Your health. Every organ of your body that may have been diagnosed as defective.

#5. Speak to your finances, your sources of income. Mention your business name and speak to it.

#6. Speak to the industry where your income is coming from to release all that is yours in that industry or sector of the economy.

#7. Speak to your nation to release its water, its minerals, its resources to you.

***

Satan told Jesus to bow down to worship him so the Lord would be given the wealth and resources of nations. What an insult! Our Lord Jesus is the Lord and Creator of all things and does not have to bow to any devil to have access to the wealth of nations if He wanted. "All things were made by Him and without Him was nothing made that was made" (John 1:3).

Jesus said Satan is a thief. We don't have to join any cult or do any rituals to have access to wealth. God gives "power to get wealth" (Deut 8:18).

Because the earth is the Lord's and the fullness thereof, and if indeed you know you are a child of God, you must know you are a global citizen wherever you are on the planet Earth.

Speak to the rock of that nation to release its resources to you.

The rock can be some departments that need to release certain things to you to enhance your status and dignity.

The rock can be a real 'he' - people who have no feeling or empathy; people who know you, who have what you need but who naturally don't have any feeling of helping anyone. God can move their hearts to release their water to you.

You don't have to be a politician to have access to the waters from the rock of your nation. Speak to the rock. Water can flow from there to reach you in your room or office. When water came out from that rock in the wilderness, both humans and their beasts drank from the water. Water can flow to your beasts, your business. We cannot continue to allow only evil politicians to be drinking the water from that rock of our nation. The rock must release its water to us. Amen.

This should not be a prayer project for just one day.

Give God worship and praise as a declaration that the earth is His and its fullness.

Prayer Session #66

EVIL PROPHECIES EXPIRE!

Matthew 2: 16-18.

> *16. Then Herod, when he saw that he was mocked of the wise men, was exceeding wroth, and sent forth, and slew all the children that were in Bethlehem, and in all the coasts thereof, from two years old and under, according to the time which he had diligently inquired of the wise men.*
>
> *17. Then was fulfilled that which was spoken by Jeremiah the prophet, saying,*
>
> *18. 'In Rama was there a voice heard, lamentation, and weeping, and great mourning, Rachel weeping for her children, and would not be comforted, because they are not.'*

There are three Old Testament prophecies that are fulfilled in Matthew 2. One is on the place of birth of the King, Jesus. (V. 4-6). The 2nd prophecy is that Africa (represented by Egypt) would be the continent to give security and cover for Jesus. Africa would preserve Jesus from the strangling efforts of the evil forces from the Middle East. Even today, Africa is the one 'preserving' Christ while the whole of Middle East (through Islam) & the western world have strangled the faith of Christ. No matter what problems the Church in Africa is facing, we are still the greatest continent preserving the Christian faith. Even in Europe, it is Africans that are holding the light of the name of Jesus.

Third prophecy in that Matthew 2 is a bad prophecy. When Herod massacred, maybe over 100 children, the Scripture says, "Then was fulfilled that which was spoken by Jeremiah the prophet, saying, 'In Rama was there a voice heard, lamentation, and weeping, and great mourning, Rachel weeping for her children, and would not be comforted, because they are not.'"

***

#1. In the name of Jesus Christ, every evil dream I ever had that has not come to pass but still waiting for an appropriate day of manifestation, expire!

***

The fact that a bad dream or prophecy came several years ago and did not come to pass does not mean it is false or will not come to pass. Jeremiah's prophecy was hanging in the air for over 600 years before it came into fulfilment.

Sometimes, a prophecy or dream doesn't make sense until it comes to pass. For example, when Jeremiah gave this prophecy around 650 BC (Jeremiah 31:15), Rachel had long died. In fact, Rachel died in Genesis 35:19 - over 1500 years before the massacre of babies in Bethlehem. So, this prophecy naturally didn't make sense.

But Jeremiah saw into the future that Rachel was weeping and mourning terribly for her children because they were slaughtered. In reality, Rachel never lost any child. She had only two children, Joseph and Benjamin, and both of them grew very old and were successful in life.

So, that prophecy didn't make sense at the time it was given. But when it happened, people understood.

The massacre of children happened in the very town where Rachel died of pains of childbirth and where she was buried.

We read in Genesis 35: 19: *"And Rachel died, and was buried in the way to Ephrath, which is Bethlehem."*

It was like the weeping of Rachel was still in the air. (Order for my e-book *WOMAN, WHY ARE YOU WEEPING?* through: jetipraise@gmail.com)

***

#2. Any bad dream I ever had and it did not make sense to me, but is still waiting in the air for manifestation, expire today - in the name of Jesus Christ.

***

Jeremiah who saw the bloodbath of Matthew 2 wasn't a false prophet. He was one of the top ten authentic prophets of God in the Bible. God started using him when he was still a teenager. And he prophesied for over 70 years.

Bad dream or prophecy may come from God. Some are not from God. When God shows something bad coming, if it is not directly from Him as a punishment over a land or person or family, then it is information about what the devil is planning to do. The information is given ahead so that people can do something to avert it.

If there are evil prophecies hanging over a nation and there are no intercessors to resist this in the spirit, those evil prophecies may come to pass. Sometimes some people prophesy by enchantments and sorcery and try to release evil spirits into the air to enforce such prophecy in order to prove that they are authentic prophets and must be respected.

***

#4. Even if a Jeremiah has prophesied war for our nation, we stand in the name of Jesus and reject it.

#5. It shall not stand. Neither shall it come to pass.

#6. Every battalion of devils from the forests, from the air, from the waters, that are getting ready to ignite the fire of war and bloodbath in our land, we bind you in the name of Jesus.

#7. Satanic army, satanic Airforce and Naval/Marine forces commissioned to trouble our nation this year, be scattered - in the name of Jesus.

#8. In your forests, we bind you there.

#9. In your waters, we bind you there.

#10. In your air, we bind you there.

***

"In Rama was there a voice heard, lamentation, and weeping, and great mourning, Rachel weeping for her children, and would not be comforted, because they are not."

***

#11. Voice of lamentation is already being heard in the land - in the North East of Nigeria and in the Middle Belt. Wives and children of soldiers and civilians are morning and lamenting because their fathers and husbands are no more. O God, arise, and help the land. Vain is the help of man.

#12. This year, there shall be no weeping in my family.

#13. I will not lose any member of my relatives.

#14. I will not mourn. I will not be mourned - in the name of Jesus.

Prayer Session #67

"I HAVE ENOUGH"

Genesis 33: 9.

And Esau said, I have enough, my brother; keep that thou hast unto thyself.

Having run away from his brother Esau and laboured in a foreign land for twenty years, Jacob brought plenty of animals and goods as gifts to appease Esau for the offence he committed. But Esau said he also had been blessed enough. "I already have plenty, my brother. Keep what you have for yourself" (NIV).

***

#1. In the name of Jesus Christ, I will have plenty enough.

***

People say human needs are insatiable. But here we see someone who declares, "I have enough. I already have plenty. I don't need any gift..."

One thing about this man is that his dad had cursed him twenty years before then. The curse was that he would serve his younger brother and would labour much before he eats. The man took his destiny in his hands and decided to succeed in spite of this curse. He had inherited some wonderful blessings of greatness from his grandpa, Abraham. But his immediate dad placed a curse of limitation on him.

After 20 years, Esau had amassed so much wealth that he said he didn't need any one's help.

***

#2. In the name of Jesus, I shall not be dependent on anyone.

***

Jacob probably thought Esau would be a poor man at this time. But he was surprised to see Esau in great wealth. Esau was so great he had 400 men as personal security (whereas his grandfather Abraham had 318).

***

#3. Those expecting me to come for their help shall be disappointed.

#4. The Lord will lift me up beyond the expectations of my enemies and colleagues – in the name of Jesus.

Prayer Session #68

BLESS MY GENERATION

Matthew: 1-17.

1. The book of the generation of Jesus Christ, the son of David, the son of Abraham.

2. Abraham begat Isaac; and Isaac begat Jacob; and Jacob begat Judas and his brethren;

3. And Judas begat Phares and Zara of Thamar; and Phares begat Esrom; and Esrom begat Aram;

4. And Aram begat Aminadab; and Aminadab begat Naasson; and Naasson begat Salmon;

5. And Salmon begat Booz of Rachab; and Booz begat Obed of Ruth; and Obed begat Jesse;

6. And Jesse begat David the king; and David the king begat Solomon of her that had been the wife of Urias;

7. And Solomon begat Roboam; and Roboam begat Abia; and Abia begat Asa;

Most readers of the Bible skip the first 17 verses of the New Testament. The portion is titled **"The book of the generation of Jesus Christ"**. This part is the Genesis, the beginning of the New Testament. This shows the line from which Jesus came in the flesh. There are 42 generations. One thing we notice in many of these 42 generations is that one person is selected from each generation. For example, we read, "Abraham begat Isaac, and Isaac begat Jacob, and Jacob begat Judah and his brethren, ... David begat Solomon, Solomon begat Rehoboam, ...etc."

Isaac was not the only child of Abraham, but it was only Isaac that was named as representing that generation. Other children were just in brackets. Jacob was not the only son of Isaac. Also, Judah was just one of the 12 sons and a daughter in the family of Jacob. But only Judah was mentioned. It was like divine 'natural selection', eliminating others as not important as far as God's plan of salvation was concerned.

David had many wives and children. But only Solomon is mentioned as representing the generation. Solomon had 1000 women many of who had children. It is possible he might have had thousands of children. But only one son was mentioned here in this "book of generations."

Usually, many of us always do pray that God will select us from our family and make us as the only great and rich person in the family that everybody would be coming to beg for food and borrow money for survival.

Such prayer is not necessary. God is more than able to make everyone great in our family. God is able to save every member of our family. There is a greatness in God that can make every member of my family great in different areas of life. John says, "And of His fullness have all we received, and grace for grace." (John 1:16). There is a fullness in Christ that is sufficient to go round.

If certain members of your family remain sinners and wicked, they may be thorns in your flesh or bring embarrassment to the family name. God did not create hell fire for any member of your family. He created Hell for Satan and his demons (Matthew 25:41). Rescue the souls of your family member who Satan is already luring to follow him to Hell.

Let us pray that as many as do not know the Lord will know Him this year.

We will pray that those who acknowledge the Lord Jesus in our family will be great. No exception. No one will be a pauper. The greatness of every member of the family is the greatness of the family.

If you pray that only you should succeed or be great in your extended or immediate family or among your siblings, you may not fully enjoy your wealth. You must be ready to bear many responsibilities which eventually will deplete your own wealth.

Moreover, if you are the only successful person in your family, you must be ready to fight some spiritual battles of envy. Your wealth or success may attract attacks that you may not have the spiritual stamina to resist or overcome.

Sometimes when you are facing challenges yourself and are not able to help at a particular time, it can be regarded by others as wickedness or stinginess.

So, let us pray:

***

#1. I thank the Lord for I know there is a greatness in You that can make my generation great.

#2. All my children shall be great in their different areas of interest - in the name of Jesus. None of them shall be a pauper or an average person. None of them shall depend on the other to feed or to survive. (Mention them by name).

#3. No member of this family will be a rebel against God.

#4. I forbid any criminality in my generation. Our family name shall not be represented in prison or in any fraudulent affair.

#5. (Pray specifically for anyone in the family having specific life challenges. Ask for God's grace and lifting.

#6. I pray for all those I know are not yet born again - that the Lord will extend His grace of salvation to them.

#7. I break the power of sin over the life of such people. I tear the veil of false religions and idolatry over their souls – in the name of Jesus.

Prayer Session #69

ON THE THIRD DAY, I WILL RISE AGAIN

Mark 10:33-34:

> *"Behold, we go up to Jerusalem; and the Son of man shall be delivered unto the chief priests, and unto the scribes; and they shall condemn him to death; and shall deliver him to the Gentiles;*

> *"And they shall mock him, and shall scourge Him, and shall spit upon him, and shall kill him, and the third day he shall rise again"*

One of the reasons why Jesus came as man is to identify with some human sufferings, give solution to human sufferings and to ultimately bring redemption of man from the cause of human misery (sin).

Jesus said in the course of doing this, He would experience mockery, shame, scourging, being spat upon and finally death.

Death is the ultimate and greatest weapon any enemy can use on man. After death, they can do nothing more. But Jesus said He would allow His enemies to do their worst. Then on the third day he would rise again.

There is a Third Day for every son of man that is connected to the divine Son of Man.

Weeping may endure for a night, joy comes in the morning. For every child of God, there is a morning for every night of mourning or weeping.

The enemy cannot stop a day from rising because the rising or the breaking of a new day is determined by the rotation of the Earth around the sun. This takes 24 hours and the speed is estimated to be about 30km per second; that is 110,000km per hour! An average aircraft travels at 800km/hr. The speed of the Earth's rotation is therefore over 137 times the speed of an aircraft. It is like the speed of an aircraft that flies from to London to New York in about 15 minutes – a journey of 8 hours!

The earth is massive and yet it is moving at such a great speed continuously. As the Earth moves, it is carrying all of us along round the sun – every day! We are all daily cruising round the Sun!

Fortunately, there is no incantation or invocation that can stop this movement of the Earth round the sun and its revolution on its own axis. No herbalist can stop this movement; no demon, no witches can stop this.

***

#1. Since it is this unstoppable movement of the Earth that determines the rising of a new day, therefore, no human being and no demon in the waters or in hell can stop my tomorrow from coming and my sun from rising. Halleluiah!

#2. If they cannot stop my tomorrow, they cannot stop my Third Day from coming.

***

For a child of God, the Third Day is the day when God starts a new beginning after the enemies might have done their worst – in bringing shame, mockery, death, etc.

***

#3. Because I was crucified with Jesus Christ and was buried with him, and rose with Him in resurrection, I declare that whatever the enemy has been attempting in my life, I will rise again.

#4. From all my afflictions, this is my Third Day. I will rise again.

#5. From all the shame and mockeries I have suffered, this is my Third Day. I will rise again.

THE FEAR OF THE ENEMY
IS YOUR THIRD DAY

The enemies eventually did their worst to Jesus. And they believed they had silenced and stopped Him forever. But they had a fear.

Matthew 27:62-66.

> *62 Now the next day, that followed the day of the preparation, the chief priests and Pharisees came together unto Pilate,*
>
> *63 Saying, Sir, we remember that that deceiver said, while he was yet alive, "AFTER THREE DAYS, I WILL RISE AGAIN."*
>
> *64 Command therefore that the sepulcher be made sure until the third day, lest his disciples come by night, and steal him away, and say unto the people, He is risen from the dead: so the last error shall be worse than the first.*
>
> *65 Pilate said unto them, Ye have a watch: go your way, make [it] as sure as ye can.*

66 So they went, and made the sepulcher sure, sealing the stone, and setting a watch.

After killing Jesus, the enemies suddenly remembered there was a prophecy of the Third Day that Jesus had given. And they felt this must not be allowed to happen. Many other prophecies had come to pass when Jesus was on earth and even at His death. But the resurrection prophecy must not come to pass.

Is there a prophecy about your life that the enemies are aware of that they are working to stop its manifestation?

Usually, most of the attacks we face in life are because there is a prophecy at stake in the air waiting for fulfillment.

Joseph faced his travails because of the prophecies in the air - the prophecies the enemies heard about.

Certain people or forces may have heard some prophecies and declarations about what you want to become. They may have eavesdropped on your prayers and may have been working against them.

Sometimes, it may even be your prayer partner that picked certain prophecies or dreams of what you will become tomorrow and begins to work against them.

To stop the prophecy of the Third Day, the enemies of Jesus received a military command to stop it. They said they would use the military and police might to "secure" the sepulcher of Jesus until the Third Day expires without fulfillment of that prophecy.

***

#6. In the name of Jesus, God's plans for my life will not expire.

***

There are four levels of death: Disease (gradual death), Death itself (cessation of physical life), Decay and Disintegration.

When death reaches the level of decay, smelling begins and all the parts of the body begin to break to pieces until everything is scattered or consumed.

Lazarus had reached decay and disintegration had started after third day. Jesus got there on the fourth day! When Jesus got there, Mary said, the third day had passed. Decay had started and he was already smelling. For her, the third day has passed. It was now too late.

But Jesus said "I am The Resurrection and the Life". He stopped the process of decay and reversed the whole thing. Lazarus came back to life and stood up!

When Jesus died, the enemy said they would supervise the decay. They would stay in front of the sepulcher that is tightly locked up and they would make sure they begin to smell the decay before they can be sure they have finally finished the destiny of Jesus.

For them, killing Jesus on the cross was not enough. He must smell in their presence before they can feel a sense of accomplishment.

Unfortunately, they could not prevent the Third Day from coming. They wanted to be sure that even if Jesus came back to life in the sepulcher, he would not be able to come out. The grave was so sealed he would have suffocated to death even if he rose up; He would have died again by hunger and suffocation. But Jesus rose and left them there!

***

#7. This year, I will rise and leave my enemies behind!

#8. In the name of Jesus, I am coming out of my sepulcher.

***

Have you been experiencing mockery?

This is your third day.

Your reputation and honor and dignity will rise again - in the name of Jesus.

Have you been scourged in life?

This is your third day.

You will rise again.

Has the enemy killed an aspect your life?

This is your third day. You will rise again.

Has a good relationship died in your life?

This is your third day. It will rise again.

Is any organ of your body dying?

Speak to it.

Before the enemy put Jesus in a sepulcher, David had spoken on behalf of Jesus several years back: *"Thou shalt not suffer (allow) your holy one to see corruption (decay). (Psalm 16:10).*

***

#9. You my body, you will not see corruption. Every decay going on in my body, let the power of resurrection reverse the process – in the name of Jesus.

#10. I will not die mentally or intellectually.

#11. I will not die financially. This is my Third day. Financially, I will rise again.

#12. Matrimonially, I will rise again.

#13. Those who think I will die in the sepulcher of bachelorhood or spinsterhood, this is my third day. I am rising from this sepulcher - in the name of Jesus.

#14. My business, you will rise again.

***

The enemies said they must sit down at the sepulcher of Jesus so that He would start rotting in their presence. They waited in vain. My enemies will wait in vain.

On the Third Day, God commissioned a mighty Angel from heaven to help in the fulfillment of that prophecy.

***

#15. Father, I ask that you commission a mighty Angel from Heaven to supervise my rising again.

#16. (Give God quality praise. He is powerful. Only He can control the rising of my sun, my tomorrow, my Third Day. Glory!)

ENDING WITH COMMUNION

(Break bread in communion tonight in your family with this prayer)

In Hebrew language, Passover is called "Pesach". It was commanded by God to remember the deliverance that God brought to His people in Egypt through Moses.

In Exodus 12, God said after the lamb "without spot or blemish" is killed, He would send his judgment on Egypt as final blow to deliver His people. It was that same night that all Israelites were delivered.

Our own Lamb, Jesus, has been killed already.

In Exodus 23, God gives seven specific promises of blessings when He blesses their bread and water:

> *25 And ye shall serve the LORD your God, and he shall bless thy bread, and thy water; and I will take sickness away from the midst of thee.*

> *26 There shall nothing cast their young, nor be barren, in thy land: the number of thy days I will fulfill.*

27 I will send my fear before thee, and will destroy all the people to whom thou shalt come, and I will make all thine enemies turn their backs unto thee.

He said He will:

i. Send an angel before you to guard you.

ii. Be an enemy to your enemies.

iii. Bless you with provision.

iv. Remove sickness from you.

v. Prevent barrenness and miscarriages.

vi. Give you a long life.

vii. Make you fruitful.

Please, activate this covenant over your family. Release these blessings upon your life and your family today. Mention the names of your family members as you release these blessings.

Ask the Lord to send His Angel to deliver all those in the hands of terrorist captors today.

Let God visit the Egypt of these terrorists and plague them. Let them release the women and men in a hurry.

Worship His Majesty.

ABOUT THE AUTHOR

Born in Lagos State, Nigeria, Moses was born again in 1980. He worked briefly as a journalist and broadcaster with the Lagos State Broadcasting Corporation.

He was among the pioneer graduates of the Ogun State University, Nigeria. He did his Master's degree in English at the University of Ibadan in 1992.

He attended Haggai Institute in Maui (Hawaii, USA) in 1997 and two years later joined the International Faculty of the Institute. He pastored for a few years but presently involves in itinerary Christian evangelistic and prayer ministries.

He has published over 15 books, some of which are published in the UK, USA and the Netherlands.

Moses Gbenu is President of Ministry of External Affairs. He is also a director and board member of Globalfilma and Nehemiah Production, Christian movie producing companies based in the UK, USA and Nigeria.

Moses and his wife, Monisola, are also involved in marriage counselling and deliverance ministrations and are blessed with four men.

For more information and testimonies, contact the author through email:

Ministry of Eternal Affairs
jetipraise@gmail.com

Printed in Great Britain
by Amazon

79447927R00169